"Anna Kress's *Heal Your Past to Manifest You* map for those ready to break free from the cha into their true power. With profound insights and practical wisdom, Kress offers a gentle reminder that there's nothing wrong with you; it's about embracing the crucial inner work needed for meaningful manifestation. A must-read for holistic healing and personal growth."

—**Jessica Baum, LMHC**, author of *Anxiously Attached*

"Anna skillfully and compassionately guides us back to feeling safe and toward our heart's desires. If you value your peace, this book is a must-read. A healing and galvanizing manual for living the life you aspire to lead."

—**Suzy Reading**, chartered psychologist, and author of *Rest to Reset*

"Anna Kress takes you on a transformative journey in *Heal Your Past to Manifest Your Future*. With chapters like 'Befriend Your Nervous System' and 'Embrace Positive Emotions,' this book offers practical insights for those aspiring to build the life of their dreams. It's a must-read for anyone seeking emotional healing and transformative growth."

—**Kristen Schwartz, MA, CTRC**, empath counselor and trauma recovery professional at Realized Empath, and author of *The Healed Empath*

"*Heal Your Past to Manifest Your Future* is a gentle yet practical and applicable guide to healing deeper-layered traumas and wounds, while simultaneously helping you develop a resilient and focused mindset to manifest a life you've always dreamed of. Anna Kress offers practical tools, strategies, and explanations that you can seamlessly integrate into your daily life. It is truly a wonderful, supportive book for anyone who is currently navigating their healing journey."

—**Kelly Vincent, PsyD**, licensed clinical psychologist, owner of Nourished Wellness Group, and author of *True You*

"*Heal Your Past to Manifest Your Future* is the only book on manifestation I would recommend. It successfully empowers people to envision and create their dream life, while also making space for the challenges and hardship they may face along the way. This book is an excellent combination of psychological research and traditional manifestation practices."

—**Whitney Goodman, LMFT**, author of *Toxic Positivity*,
and founder of Calling Home

"*Heal Your Past to Manifest Your Future* is a transformative guidebook that empowers readers to integrate past wounds and create a fulfilling future. Through practical exercises and inspiring insights, Anna Kress offers a trauma-informed road map to process old pain, embrace new challenges, and unlock limitless potential. This book is a ray of light for those ready to get unstuck and step into who they came here to be."

—**Britt Frank, LSCSW, SEP**, licensed psychotherapist, and
author of *The Science of Stuck* and *The Getting Unstuck Workbook*

"Reading this book, I couldn't help but say, 'Yes, yes, YES!' to every single page. Anna Kress has created the ultimate self-help book for the messy and magnificent times we are living in. Blending metaphysical practices with cutting-edge psychology and somatic knowledge, *Heal Your Past to Manifest Your Future* demonstrates how you can only manifest what you feel *safe enough* to have. If you're seeking your best life, this is your guide!"

—**Kris Ferraro**, international energy healer; speaker;
and author of *Manifesting, Your Difference Is Your Strength*,
and *Energy Healing*

Heal Your Past to Manifest Your Future

Trauma-Informed Practices to Release Emotional Blocks and Open to Life's Possibilities

ANNA KRESS, PSYD

REVEAL PRESS
AN IMPRINT OF NEW HARBINGER PUBLICATIONS

Publisher's Note

This publication is designed to provide accurate and authoritative information in regard to the subject matter covered. It is sold with the understanding that the publisher is not engaged in rendering psychological, financial, legal, or other professional services. If expert assistance or counseling is needed, the services of a competent professional should be sought.

NEW HARBINGER PUBLICATIONS is a registered trademark of New Harbinger Publications, Inc.

New Harbinger Publications is an employee-owned company.

"Moving Between Stress and Support" exercise adapted from "Step 3. Pendulation and Containment: The Innate Power of Rhythm," from *In an Unspoken Voice: How the Body Releases Trauma and Restores Goodness* by Peter A. Levine, published by North Atlantic Books. Copyright © 2010 by Peter A. Levine. Used by permission of publisher.

"Go on a Glimmer Quest" exercise adapted from *Polyvagal Exercises for Safety and Connection: 50 Client-Centered Practices* by Deb Dana. Copyright © 2020 by Deborah A. Dana. Used by permission of W. W. Norton & Company, Inc.

Cover design by Amy Daniel; Acquired by Georgia Kolias; Edited by Gretel Hakanson

Library of Congress Cataloging-in-Publication Data on file

FSC
www.fsc.org
MIX
Paper from
responsible sources
FSC® C008955

Printed in the United States of America

26   25   24

10   9   8   7   6   5   4   3   2   1   First Printing

For your inner child.
May they feel safe enough to dream bigger and live louder.

Contents

Introduction

The dilemma is that unresolved trauma forces us to repeat what we have done before. New and creative assemblages of possibilities will not easily occur to us.

—Dr. Peter A. Levine, *Waking the Tiger*

You may have picked this book up because you've heard of manifesting and wondered if it really is possible to turn your dreams and desires into reality. If you've had a difficult or traumatic past, you might struggle with this idea. After all, it's hard to believe you can positively impact your reality when you've had painful, disempowering experiences. You may have even wondered why bad things happened to you in the first place. As a psychologist, I'm here to tell you that we don't cause or attract our trauma. Trauma is devastating and not our fault. We don't get to choose our past. But we do have the power to release the emotional pain we've been carrying and to change our future. That's where manifesting comes in.

I discovered manifesting as a teen living in poverty in a tough inner city. When I was a child in the early 1980s, my father fought to democratize Poland as an activist in the solidarity movement. Eventually he was arrested and held as a political prisoner. After a few years, he was released, and we sought asylum at a refugee camp in Germany. When I was seven, we came to the United States as political refugees. I had to learn the language quickly and adjust to the harsh reality of navigating inner city life. To say it was a lot would be an understatement.

By the time I was a teenager, I felt hopeless and tired of living in survival mode, wondering when I could finally come up for air. That's when one of my friends moved away to an idyllic, affluent suburb and I started visiting her on the weekends. I couldn't believe how different her new reality was. It was virtually crime-free, uneventful, and distinctly lacking in concrete. Until then, I thought tree-lined streets and white picket fences only existed in the movies. The disparities between her town and my city couldn't be more obvious. She had green spaces, resourced schools, safety, and opportunities. Most importantly, the town was home to a small used bookstore. It was there that I fell in love with personal growth books and first learned about manifesting.

Setting goals and working on manifesting them gave me a newfound sense of control. My friend's new life showed me what was possible, and manifestation teachings and practices gave me a path to get there. I discovered that as soon as we're finally given a chance to experience agency, we can become hopeful and resilient even before our situation changes. Positive images of the future can carry us forward. This was both comforting and intoxicating. Every day I set intentions, visualized, wrote affirmations and scripts, meditated, worked on my mindset, and took inspired action. It felt like an unfair secret shortcut to achieving the life I desired. It was simple and fun, and it worked. My life started to miraculously change. Synchronicities and opportunities began to show up. Life became easier. Things worked out for me more often than not. The goals I visualized came to fruition regularly. People responded differently to me. For years I rode this manifestation high.

But what goes up must come down. I was a postdoctoral fellow at Princeton University when I found myself struggling with manifestation beliefs and practices. After years of studying spirituality in women who were experiencing infertility for my doctoral dissertation research, I was now experiencing infertility myself. Studying trust in the Universe was one thing, having it tested so shortly after felt like a cruel cosmic joke.

I felt lost, and manifesting, as I understood it, seemed painfully out of reach. Positive thinking became impossible as my carefully curated mindset started to crumble, and my nervous system was no longer on board with sitting and visualizing. It was then that I realized I needed a more robust approach to manifesting, one that integrated psychology and could help me move through the emotional block I was experiencing.

In this book, I'll be sharing some of my own foibles with manifesting—mostly in the form of trying to force things for all the wrong reasons—and how I came to have the relaxed, trusting openness I have today. I'll take you through the three-step process that I've used with myself and my clients to get unstuck and start manifesting successfully—even if you've experienced trauma.

Understanding Trauma

Emotional blocks are the unprocessed—or trapped—emotions that keep us stuck and from having or doing the things we really want in life. We can try to override them with willpower, bypass them with spirituality, or outrun them. But eventually, we must face them if we want things to change on a deeper level. Over the years as a trauma therapist, my approach to manifesting has both softened and sharpened. I've learned that facing manifestation-related emotional blocks can be done in a safe and gentle way when it's trauma-informed. By healing and releasing stuck emotions, we can begin to trust the process of manifesting and open up to new possibilities. I've also had a taste of harmful manifestation beliefs and practices and have made it my mission to advocate for a psychologically responsible approach that takes mental health, diversity, and trauma into account.

Trauma is caused by distressing events that exceed our ability to cope, disrupt our functioning, and often have long-term negative physical and mental health consequences. There are different forms of trauma, and all can impact our beliefs about whether it's possible or safe to manifest what we want.

The most commonly understood form of trauma is post-traumatic stress disorder (PTSD). PTSD is sometimes called shock trauma because it refers to the presence of symptoms after a single traumatic event that is frightening or overwhelming, such as an act of violence, a car accident, a natural disaster, or a death.

Complex post-traumatic stress disorder (C-PTSD), also called complex trauma, is an equally serious form of trauma that you might be less familiar with. Complex trauma refers to the presence of symptoms after experiencing prolonged, repeated trauma. Complex trauma often stems from trauma and chronic stress in childhood. For example, C-PTSD can occur when children have adverse childhood experiences.

There are ten adverse childhood experiences identified in the groundbreaking research on the negative physical and mental health effects of adverse childhood experiences (ACEs).[1] These include:

1. Emotional abuse

2. Physical abuse

3. Sexual abuse

4. Emotional neglect

5. Physical neglect

6. Loss of parent (including separation, divorce, or death)

7. Domestic violence

8. Family member with addiction

9. Family member with mental illness

10. Family member in prison.

In addition to the ACEs categories, therapists assess for many other traumatic events including: a parent with PTSD or C-PTSD; a mother who experienced postpartum depression; a lack of emotional safety in the family; a lack of respect for boundaries by family members; competition with siblings for limited parental attention; chronic poverty; serious injury; witnessing violence; repeated discrimination or bullying; chronic rejection, shaming, or being dismissed; and caregivers with characteristics of narcissistic or borderline personality disorder.[2]

When complex trauma occurs in childhood, it can also be referred to as developmental trauma. If our caregivers are unable to meet our needs to feel seen, safe, and soothed, and we develop an insecure attachment style, this type of complex trauma is sometimes referred to as attachment trauma. Complex trauma can also occur in adulthood as a result of ongoing distressing experiences, such as domestic violence, prolonged captivity, refugee trauma, and systemic racism.[3] Complex trauma that is passed down through generations is called intergenerational trauma, inherited trauma, or a legacy burden. People who heal and carve a new path that ends the passing down of inherited trauma are called cycle breakers.

There is one other type of trauma I'd like to bring to your attention since it can happen in the context of manifestation communities: religious trauma. Unfortunately, there are some charismatic spiritual teachers who groom unsuspecting newcomers and indoctrinate them into particularly harmful belief systems. While spiritual abuse and cults are beyond the scope of this book, in chapter 9, I'll point out some red flags to look for when assessing whether a spiritual manifestation belief, practice, or teacher is harmful.

In addition to helping you identify spiritual abuse, this book will give you a trauma-informed approach to manifesting by acknowledging that social conditions perpetuate trauma and block access to resources and opportunities. Oppression is pervasive and comes in many forms. Having privileges shouldn't be mistaken for, or presented as, manifesting, and marginalization and lack of privileges aren't indicators of poor manifesting abilities. To blame people for their unfair circumstances is both abusive and retraumatizing. To be trauma-informed, we need to be intentional about how we talk about trauma and sensitive to the impact it might have.

For example, although some trauma therapists still make the distinction between *big-T* trauma and *small-t* trauma, these concepts can be misleading. Adverse life experiences, formerly called small-t traumas, such as chronically feeling misunderstood or like we can never measure up to a narcissistic parent's expectations, can be just as detrimental to our functioning and neurobiology as life-threatening trauma. The repeated exposure to emotional distress can feel unmanageable, especially if we don't have a supportive person in our lives who can help us regulate our nervous system and buffer the stress. The expression "death by a thousand cuts" refers to how repeated wounds like these can add up. The more dysregulated and helpless we feel in the situation, the more likely we are to experience it as trauma. The reality is that trauma is not about the event, but about our internal response and the negative long-term effects on our body and mind. Many people who have suffered from what was once called small-t trauma struggle with symptoms they don't understand and blame themselves as a result. They don't identify as trauma survivors and don't feel entitled to seek help. It's important to acknowledge that there is no judgment when it comes to which traumas are significant and worthy of our attention. What matters is how trauma affects us.

How Trauma May Be Affecting You

Despite their differences, all traumas have basic features in common. Trauma pioneer Dr. Janina Fisher calls these features "the living legacy of trauma."[4] Since the stress of traumatic experiences shuts down the verbal memory areas of our brains, we might only remember fragments of the experience or not realize that our bodies are remembering when we have a strong emotional or physical reaction to a trigger. Rather than a coherent narrative of traumatic events or conditions, the experience usually shows up in the ways our body and mind adapted to manage the stress. Consider the following difficulties that Fisher identifies.[5] Which ones might be showing up in your life as a result of trauma?

- Hypervigilance and mistrust

- Loss of a sense of the future and hopelessness

- Shame and worthlessness

- Emotional overwhelm

- Anxiety and panic attacks

- Depression

- Numbing

- Irritability

- Insomnia and nightmares

- Flashbacks (including emotional flashbacks, which are sudden, overwhelming regressions to a feeling-state of being traumatized)

- Few or no memories

- Loss of interest

- Trouble concentrating

- Substance abuse or eating disorders

- Chronic pain, including headaches

- Feeling unreal or out of body (dissociation)

- Loss of a sense of "who I am"

- Self-destructive behavior

Trauma has a lasting impact and can affect your ability to imagine and create the positive outcomes you want in life. In *The Body Keeps the Score: Brain, Mind, and Body in the Healing of Trauma*, trauma expert Dr. Bessel van der Kolk talks about a study in which he and his colleagues used an instrument called a Thematic Apperception Test (TAT) with traumatized children.[6] The TAT involves showing relatively benign photos to participants and asking them to describe what they see. The traumatized children in the study saw only "disastrous outcomes" in common images of everyday life.[7] Meanwhile, van der Kolk concluded that the children in the study who had not been abused "still trusted in an essentially benign universe; they could imagine ways out of bad situations."[8]

I believe that manifestation practices can help you imagine positive outcomes and ways out of challenging situations, but only if your nervous system and the traumatized parts of yourself are on board. It's a shift that requires working on healing trauma and modifying manifestation teachings and practices to be trauma-sensitive. This book will show you how to do just that with my three-step process: regulate, reparent, rewire.

How This Book Can Help

I suggest you read this book in the order it's presented because each chapter builds on the last. First our body needs to feel safe, then our inner child needs to feel safe, and last, we can start to invite in new possibilities through manifesting. It's a natural progression from surviving, to finding safety, to thriving.

In the first part of the book, I'll show you how to regulate your emotions and nervous system so they support what you're trying to manifest. In the middle chapters, I'll cover reparenting wounded younger parts of yourself using a revolutionary trauma therapy called Internal Family Systems (IFS). IFS will also be used to work with the protective parts of your personality that oppose each other's goals and keep you stuck. We'll also look at healing your attachment style, including your attachment style to the Universe so it's easier to trust the manifestation process. In the last third of the book, I'll share manifestation practices that can help you rewire the feelings you have associated with your goals and increase your ability to believe in new possibilities. You'll learn some of my unique techniques, including the one that helped me get pregnant. There is also a website for this book, http://www.newharbinger.com/53042, where you can find free tools and resources to support your journey.

I invite you to think about manifesting as a supportive path to thriving. I believe this is true, but only if the teachings and practices have mental health in mind. The dominant trend in manifesting has always been to focus on an extreme version of positivity at all costs, even if it's at the expense of compassion for ourselves or others. Such approaches can leave us stranded in toxic shame when we experience any difficulty or can't reach the touted results. I hope that this trend is changing as we become a more trauma-informed culture, and sometimes I believe that a quiet revolution is already underway.

For now, my hope is that this book is a friendly guide for you, dear reader. I know that when you start to release the pain you've been carrying, you can let go of what was and listen for what wants to emerge. Expansion and possibility become inevitable. Lastly, I know that manifesting shouldn't be reserved for the privileged few who've already tasted success and can think positive thoughts all hours of the day. Its teachings and practices should be inclusive, and anyone who is marginalized or traumatized should be able to use them without fear that they will be blamed for their unfair or unfortunate circumstances.

I want you to safely get to know previously cutoff feelings and parts of yourself. I want you to see that within you, there's a very still eternal self that can hold feelings tenderly and alchemize them. I want to show you what's possible when you lean into self-compassion and self-trust. I know what you're capable of because I believe in you, and I hope that soon you will too.

No matter what you've been through, trauma-informed practices can help you turn pain into possibility and manifest a positive future.

CHAPTER 1

Ditch Toxic Positivity to Accept Yourself and Your Emotions

Healthy positivity means making space for both reality and hope.

—Whitney Goodman, *Toxic Positivity*

Your story may be similar to Christine's. She first learned about manifesting through a popular life coach's social media account. The coach had a large following and posted testimonials from clients who manifested abundance, romance, health, and career success using her methods. Christine was eager to try the techniques to manifest a romantic relationship. For years, she had a pattern of dating emotionally immature men who only wanted to be in a "situationship." She was thirty-four and ready to start a family. Longing for a conscious and committed partner, Christine was willing to do whatever it took. She learned about the Law of Attraction—the idea that energy with a certain vibration attracts energy with a similar vibration—and tried to avoid any negative thoughts or emotions that might attract painful dating circumstances.

Christine signed up for the coach's master class and did all the exercises, even though they significantly increased her anxiety. Trying to suppress her constant stream of negative thoughts and replace them with positive ones wasn't just daunting, it made her hypervigilant and terrified. There were just so many worried, doubting, and hopeless thoughts. What if she let too many slip by? Would her dream slip by as well? Whenever the coach instructed her to close her eyes and visualize the type of relationship she wanted, she could feel her heart race. She wanted to do a good job, but something about sitting still and looking within made her feel unsafe. By the end of the class, Christine felt discouraged. She wasn't seeing any results. When she asked the coach why she felt more anxious and wasn't manifesting what she desired, the coach told her it indicated a lack of positivity. Eager to please, Christine accepted the explanation. She continued trying to improve her mindset—without any results for the next three years. By the time she saw me for therapy, she felt more anxious and depressed than she did before discovering manifesting.

Like Christine, you may have encountered manifestation teachings and practices and wondered if they could work for you. *The good news is they can.* Manifestation teachings can expand your sense of what's possible and give you exciting, powerful tools to achieve the goals that, up until now, may have felt out of reach. But you might get the impression that manifesting isn't for you if you have a history of trauma or mental health symptoms. After all, the main message behind manifestation teachings is that positivity is crucial for attracting what you want. Whether it's positive thoughts, emotions, beliefs, or expectations, most teachings consider positivity necessary for successful manifesting.

The problem with overemphasizing positivity is that being positive isn't simply a matter of willpower or choice for someone with a history of trauma or a mood disorder. Struggles with thoughts, beliefs, and emotions can be challenging. Symptoms are not fleeting; they are *persistent and distressing.* Negative emotional states endure and make it extremely difficult to experience positive thoughts or emotions. Moreover, symptoms often include *persistent and exaggerated* negative beliefs or expectations. These beliefs and expectations can be about ourselves, others, and even the world. Under all our positive intentions and desires, we might believe that we are worthless, no one can be trusted, and the world is unsafe.

You won't recover from trauma and mood disorders simply by replacing *persistent* negative thoughts, emotions, beliefs, and expectations with positive ones. Unlike occasional self-critical thoughts and gloomy moods, trauma and mood disorder symptoms are intrusive, involuntary, and unwanted. Therefore, they don't respond to surface-level solutions offered by life coaches like the one Christine followed.

When you venture into popular manifestation teachings and practices, you'll often hear the message that happiness and positive thoughts are a choice. While it might be well-intentioned, this is an example of *toxic positivity*. Toxic positivity is the idea that we should have a positive mindset rather than validate or experience emotional pain. While positivity in the face of adversity is sometimes helpful, trying to be positive in an excessive or overgeneralized way isn't an effective strategy for relieving our suffering. Even when well-intentioned, toxic positivity can intensify painful emotions and exacerbate symptoms rather than support or heal them.

Here are examples of toxic positivity. Some of these are phrases you might have heard before (and maybe even said to try to support others). Some are beliefs you may have internalized.

- Good vibes only.

- Look on the bright side.

- You should practice gratitude.

- Other people have it worse.

- Just think positive thoughts.

- Don't worry, be happy.

- You should forgive people who hurt you.

- Choose thoughts that make you feel better.

- To attract what you want, you need to feel good.

Healthy positivity supports both a healing journey and manifesting. But the toxic positivity expressed in these statements doesn't make us feel any better. In fact, it makes us want to isolate because we feel ashamed when we can't live up to this idealized version of happiness. According to therapist Whitney Goodman, author of *Toxic Positivity: Keeping It Real in a World Obsessed with Being Happy*, toxic positivity makes us feel like failures.[9] Healthy positivity, on the other hand, is genuine and doesn't deny a range of emotions. The research agrees. Studies show that overemphasizing happiness and pleasant emotions can make us obsess over failures and unpleasant emotions, causing more stress in the long run.[10]

Spot the Difference

This exercise will give you some practice spotting the difference between toxic and healthy positivity. For each statement, identify whether it is an example of someone experiencing toxic positivity or healthy positivity. Keep in mind that one makes us feel worse and the other has the potential to make us feel better. Answers and explanations follow.

1. I must write in my gratitude journal three times a day or else I won't be successful.

2. I feel anxious right now, but I can show myself compassion and use self-care tools to feel better.

3. I'll never manifest what I want if I keep letting myself think negative thoughts.

4. I got bad news, and it's understandable that I feel disappointed. I'll call my sister because she is a good listener.

5. If I don't feel joyful all the time, I'll block my blessings.

6. It didn't work out this time, and I need to recover. I'll spend some time healing and then try again—I know I can do it.

7. If I put my attention only on things I like and appreciate, my problems will all go away.

Questions 1, 3, 5, and 7 are examples of toxic positivity. In question 1, gratitude is turned into a practice that is filled with pressure and guilt. In question 3, an unrealistic standard is applied to negative thinking. We all have negative thoughts, and trying to suppress them is not an effective strategy. (We'll discuss more effective strategies for managing thoughts and feelings later in this chapter.) In question 5, there is an unrealistic desire to experience only positive emotions and increased anxiety about natural, human emotions because of the belief that they repel blessings. And in question 7, the idea that we can solve all our problems by focusing only on positive things is toxic because denial can lead to real consequences (as in a medical issue getting worse without proper attention and care).

Meanwhile, questions 2, 4, and 6 acknowledge feelings with compassion and demonstrate that while it's not always possible to choose happiness, we can deliberately engage in practices that support our emotional wellness and resilience.

It can be a huge relief to recognize toxic positivity and walk away from it in favor of healthy positivity. I do want to caution you that not everyone who teaches manifestation or engages in manifestation practices believes that positivity can, at times, be harmful. They might try to use mindset language or spiritual concepts that aren't trauma-sensitive. Instead of helping you, they get you to question or blame yourself. This is where firm boundaries will serve you well. You can walk away from teachings and practices that are not trauma-informed and are ultimately disempowering, even if they seem popular or come from a charismatic teacher or coach.

Manifestation Myth Busting: "You Must Be Positive No Matter What"

Let's take a close look at three manifestation myths that come out of toxic positivity. This will help you start to recognize and question ideas that could have a negative impact on your mental health.

Myth. If you want to manifest your desires, you should just *choose* to be happy.

Trauma-informed perspective. The idea that "happiness is a choice" is an ableist example of toxic positivity that perpetuates stigma around mental health. Emotional wellness is much more complex and is not sustainably achieved through willpower. We can, however, improve our self-care, accept setbacks, seek professional help when needed, use proven mental health tools, and make progress toward feeling better.

Myth. If the Law of Attraction says that you attract everything, then it means you attracted your trauma.

Trauma-informed perspective. One spiritual belief cannot possibly explain everything. There are many other spiritual beliefs (including many other laws of the Universe) out there concerning why things happen to people. Traumas and tragedies happen to people regardless of positivity. Please don't limit your spirituality to this one belief or overgeneralize it and blame yourself for trauma.

Myth. Since your thoughts create things, you must think positively all the time.

Trauma-informed perspective. Not only is constant positive thinking impossible, trying to suppress negative thoughts is associated with an increase in mental health symptoms.[11] It's more important to have a positive relationship to your thought process, as we'll explore in this chapter, without the added fear of a negative consequence. Also, manifesting isn't just about your thoughts. The strategies in this book don't rely on rigid positive thinking.

You Don't Have to Be Perfect

In many manifestation circles, there is a pressure to maintain positive emotions at all costs and to make it look like the task is simple. Displaying confidence and ease are encouraged while expressing doubt and admitting struggles are discouraged. My first true encounter with this type of pressure was the year I was a postdoctoral fellow at Princeton University. Every day, I sat across from high-achieving students who struggled with mental health. I'd interned at family counseling centers, clinics, psychiatric hospitals, and college counseling centers until that point, but this was different. My psychotherapy clients at Princeton didn't just struggle with mental health; they had the added pressure of needing to appear happy. After all, they achieved the nearly impossible goal of attending a top university. They got the golden ticket. But many were already burned-out by the time they got there. In high school, everyone around them had insisted that their sacrifices would all be worth it when they got to college. For most, however, trying to keep up with a whole campus full of extremely competitive students was a culture shock. The result was masking painful feelings and hiding hard work.

Princeton wasn't the only elite university where students experienced this phenomenon. Duke University coined the term *effortless perfection* to describe the pressure to display confidence and ease, regardless of actual feelings and struggles. Many other schools had their own version, including "Penn Face" at the University of Pennsylvania. Fortunately, college campuses have responded to the national college mental health crisis by prioritizing mental health. They try to create a culture where students are more comfortable talking about their struggles. I believe that manifestation circles, however, are still grappling with their own version of effortless perfection.

You may have experienced this. In some group coaching situations, this pressure creates a competitive environment. Both coaches and students feel the pressure to look like a "good manifestor" who has the power to attract anything they want as a result of their ceaseless positivity. The happiness bar is set so impossibly high that everyone falls short and lives in fear of being discovered. They might admit experiencing a challenge, but quickly follow up with how they managed to overcome it and are now happier than ever. The irony is that they often sacrifice basic mental health by trying to project an image of ideal mental health.

While manifestation culture still encourages masking emotions and hiding struggles, healthy positivity isn't perfect, and you don't have to be either. Christine wished she could get back the years she spent beating herself up and going back to the same coach over and over. She didn't realize that there were proven mental health tools that could help her feel better. Her healing became a catalyst for manifesting the committed romantic relationship she wanted. Most importantly, Christine was surprised to discover that the transformation she was looking for didn't require her to exude effortless perfection or push herself to change. Instead, it asked her to be gentler and more accepting.

The Power of Acceptance

There was a time when changing thoughts and feelings was the goal of many psychotherapy models. Thanks to decades of research on mindfulness-based therapy techniques, that time has long since passed. We now know that trying to suppress and avoid negative thoughts and feelings has a rebound effect that intensifies and prolongs them. In research this is called *experiential avoidance*, and it's associated with the development and maintenance of anxiety,[12] depression,[13] substance use disorders,[14] obsessive-compulsive disorder,[15] and post-traumatic stress disorder.[16] The modern perspective is that it is much more powerful to change our *relationship* to thoughts and feelings than to try to change our negative thoughts or feelings.

Changing your relationship to thoughts and feelings means that you no longer try to control them, suppress them, or fight with them. It means that you accept them as an experience you are having, rather than identifying with them. This space is created by becoming a nonjudgmental observer. When you're a nonjudgmental observer, you don't automatically buy into your thoughts and feelings and act on them. You get curious about them and let them come and go. With practice, acceptance helps you regulate your feelings, which reduces mental health symptoms.

Sadly, many manifestation coaches aren't trained in mental health and pass their lack of knowledge along to students, teaching them that they should suppress negative thoughts and emotions and replace them with positive ones. To make matters more confusing, they usually also recommend mindfulness—nonjudgmental awareness and acceptance of experience—which completely contradicts suppressing and changing thoughts and emotions. Let's clear things up by looking at how we can apply mindfulness-based acceptance to our thoughts and feelings.

Accepting Your Thoughts

We all have a natural *negativity bias* that makes us overfocus on potential threats and ignore anything neutral and positive so we can stay safe. If you've experienced trauma, you can become hypervigilant and see even the neutral or positive as potential threats. Your thoughts then reflect this sense of ongoing danger. Add to that any beliefs you've developed from traumatic experiences—such as *nothing good ever happens to me*—and it's understandable that a history of trauma leads to persistent negative thoughts. You are not a negative person. Instead, your neurobiology is trying to protect you. It is physical and unconscious. And you can't override it through willpower and determination. Instead, it is useful to have some tools to manage negative thoughts daily.

The following exercises will help you develop the ability to notice your negative thoughts and detach from them. They are examples of an acceptance and commitment therapy (ACT) technique called *defusion*. Rather than being merged with your thoughts, defusion can help you observe your thinking process from the perspective of a witness. By relating to your thinking in this way, you'll find that your negative thoughts become less believable.

Leaves Floating in a Stream

This basic mindfulness meditation can be practiced any time to get comfortable with letting thoughts come and go. I invite you to read the instructions below first and then decide if you want to give it a try. It is typically done with closed eyes, but a trauma-sensitive modification is to give yourself the option to keep your eyes open (and maybe rest them gently on a spot in the room).

Imagine that you're sitting by a stream and watching your thoughts go by on leaves in the stream. One by one, put your thought (or an image if no words come to mind) on a leaf and let it float away and drift out of sight. Some thoughts will be recurring visitors that appear repeatedly, and that's okay. Don't try to change them or get rid of them. Allow them to come and go at their own pace. Continue the meditation for three to five minutes. Set a timer if you find it helpful. It's okay (and normal) if your mind drifts away during the meditation; just bring your attention back to the stream gently.

Play with this exercise regularly to get used to the idea that you are not your thoughts; you are the observer of your thought process. The more you practice, the easier it will be for you to not get fused with your thoughts. You can listen to a recording of this meditation at the website for this book, http://www.newharbinger.com/53042.

Label Your Thoughts as Thoughts

Instead of dwelling on a distressing thought, observe your mind and label what's happening. For example, you might notice that you're having judgmental or critical thoughts. Rather than saying, "I'm worthless," you can say, "I'm having the thought that I am worthless." As you might already notice, this statement just hits differently. It's less about you and more about the way your mind operates by judging and worrying when your nervous system is in survival mode. Here are some other ways to label thoughts by describing what your mind is doing.

- *I notice that I'm having the thought that _____.*

- *My mind is having a _____ thought.*

- *I notice a lot of _____ thoughts coming up.*

- *That's interesting; my mind is having a _____ thought.*

- *I'm having the thought that _____.*

Now that we've looked at how you can practice mindful acceptance of your thoughts, we'll explore mindful acceptance of emotions. But before we proceed, let's talk about a manifesting practice centered around emotions that does more harm than good.

Stop Ranking Emotions—Feel Them Instead

If you have explored different manifestation teachings, you've probably stumbled upon scales that rank emotions depending on their supposed level of vibration. The purpose of these scales is to show which emotions to strive for and which ones to try to avoid in order to be a successful manifestor. For example, peace and joy are considered magnetic, high vibration emotions on the top of the list. Meanwhile, grief and fear are considered repellent, low vibration emotions on the bottom of the list.

On your road to successful manifesting, I urge you to ignore this type of advice. *There is no evidence to show that ranking emotions actually helps us feel better.* Instead, it promotes an unhealthy judgment-based relationship to emotions that can backfire.

Here are some things to keep in mind about emotions:

- Research shows that having a full range of emotions—called *emodiversity*—is good for you because it can prevent you from having either too much of one emotion or having one emotion for too long.[17]

- Avoiding so-called negative emotions can have a rebound effect, where you get more of what you're trying to avoid.

Emotions offer information about what is happening inside of you. Sometimes they have an important message about something that needs your attention in the present. Other times, they are an alarm that is triggered repeatedly, even when you are safe, to let you know that an old wound needs to be healed. When you ignore your emotions or try to get rid of them, you miss their message. Unfortunately, most of us have not been taught to approach emotions this way. We've learned that they're something we shouldn't feel. But when you accept and respect your emotions, you are in a better position to learn from them, regulate them, and release them.

Permission to Feel

Take a few minutes to journal and reflect on your experience with emotions growing up. Allow yourself to skip questions if they feel too triggering right now.

- What did your family say about emotions?

- Which emotions were allowed in your house?

- Who was allowed to express emotions, and who wasn't? Did gender play a role?

- How did others react when you expressed emotions? Did your family try to help you regulate your emotions?

- How were emotions handled in your school?

- If you participated in a spiritual or religious community, how did they talk about emotions?

- What did you learn about emotions from media (including social media) growing up?

We receive a lot of messages about emotions growing up and from popular culture, and these messages often turn into beliefs and judgments about which feelings are acceptable. To make matters worse, manifestation teachers can further influence these beliefs and judgments by promoting toxic positivity and the ranking of emotions. It's no surprise that many of us develop strong judgments toward our own emotions—judgments that can increase our suffering.

Secondary emotions, or what are sometimes referred to as *meta-emotions*, are what psychologists call our feelings about our feelings. A primary emotion is an emotion that comes first; a secondary emotion is the emotion that follows it. For example, if you are sad because the relationship you want hasn't manifested yet, sadness is the primary emotion. If you believe that sadness is a negative emotion that will repel what you are trying to manifest, then fear might be your secondary emotion. Now, in addition to sadness, you have fear to regulate, process, and release. This is how easy it is to allow our judgments and beliefs about emotions to create more challenging emotions.

Secondary emotions are the reason it is important to not judge emotions on your journey to manifesting your dreams. If you get caught up with trying to get rid of so-called negative emotions, you'll only have more challenging emotions to manage. If, instead, you accept your emotions as natural and normal, there's a very high probability that your secondary emotions will be more pleasant and you'll be on your way to actually feeling better. For example, if you feel sad because the romantic relationship you want hasn't manifested yet, but you accept the sadness as understandable and worthy of compassion, your secondary emotion might be peace or comfort rather than fear.

In other words, our secondary emotions—our feelings about our feelings—can tip our original emotion in either a harmful or a healing direction. You might even say that we have a higher vibration whenever we practice an accepting attitude toward our emotions!

Name Your Emotions

This activity will help you accept your emotions and regulate them so they feel less threatening. Therapists model healthy ways to relate to emotions in the way we speak about them by referring to them as "painful" or "challenging" and avoiding "negative" whenever possible. Therapists also encourage clients to name their emotions (sad, afraid, joyful, irritated). This is called *affect labeling*, and there is ample research to show that it helps us regulate our emotions by deactivating the part of the brain that initiates a stress response. The more specific we get, which is called *emotional granularity*,[18] the better. As Dr. Daniel Siegel says, when it comes to a feeling, if you can name it, you can tame it. Try the following labeling activity when you notice an emotion come up:

- Check in and notice any emotion you are currently experiencing.

- Label the emotion (anxiety, sadness, irritability, boredom, frustration, and so on).

- See if you can get a little more specific (for example, rather than irritated, you might realize that you're actually overwhelmed).

- Be sure to state your feeling as an experience rather than something you identify with ("I notice a feeling of anxiety," or "I'm experiencing anxiety," rather than "I am anxious").

- Try labeling and describing your emotion out loud to see if it's helpful.

Once you label an emotion, it's easier to see if it requires soothing, regulating, or healing. In later chapters, we'll discuss different ways to work with emotions. For now, just start getting into the habit of labeling them.

Keep in mind that accepting emotions doesn't necessarily mean acting on them. If you believe an action is needed, make sure it's aligned with your values rather than driven by an unregulated emotional urge. For example, if you feel angry, you might realize you need to set a boundary with someone. Deciding to set the boundary in a healthy way when you feel less emotionally charged would be an example of a response, rather than reaction. In other words, don't suppress your emotions, but do manage your reactions.

Acceptance Leads to Transcendence

Here is a paradox of mental health: When we accept our thoughts and emotions and release the pressure to make them positive, we allow ourselves an opportunity to transcend them. Sometimes, this means we have an easier time connecting to our divine nature. Other times, it simply means our nervous system relaxes long enough to release the survival thoughts and emotions that seemed so urgent and believable just moments before.

While transcendence feels good, the deeper healing you'll learn about in this book will help you avoid a potential pitfall of both mindfulness and manifesting: *spiritual bypassing.* Coined by psychologist Dr. John Welwood in the 1980s, spiritual bypassing refers to the use of spiritual ideas and practices to avoid facing unresolved emotional issues and psychological wounds.

By accepting our thoughts and emotions, *and* healing emotional issues and psychological wounds, we can release emotional blocks keeping us from the life of our dreams. Christine experienced this when she stopped buying into toxic positivity and learned to accept herself and her emotions. She realized that her adverse experiences in childhood led to complex trauma and that her symptoms didn't make her a "negative" person incapable of manifesting successfully. Christine manifested her dreams in a trauma-informed way. She released emotional burdens and felt lighter than ever. By healing her internal experience, rather than bypassing it, she started to authentically thrive in her outer world. This meant that the things she wanted to manifest for years suddenly became not only more accessible, but also natural.

A New Way to Manifest

You, too, can unlock the magic of manifesting by making peace with all your emotions. You can shift out of survival mode into thriving and successfully creating and manifesting. Once you ditch toxic positivity to practice more acceptance, you are free to try manifestation techniques without the added fear of doing it wrong. In the next chapter, we'll start with some fun manifestation techniques to help you develop the courage to ask for what you want and to trust in the process despite feelings of uncertainty—two things that are usually compromised after trauma.

Take-Home Points

- Our thoughts are often mood-based and biased.

- Difficult and unpleasant emotions are a normal part of everyone's experience.

- Accepting our thoughts and emotions doesn't mean believing them; it means treating them as experiences we can observe with space and treat with compassion.

- When we accept our thoughts and emotions and release the pressure to make them positive, we allow ourselves an opportunity to transcend them.

CHAPTER 2

Begin to Ask, Trust, and Say Yes to the Universe

Of course, the best way to have all your intentions realized is to align your intentions with the cosmic intent, to create harmony between what you intend and what the universe intends for you.

—Dr. Deepak Chopra, *The Spontaneous Fulfillment of Desire*

Now that you are on your way to greater acceptance of thoughts and emotions, let's look at manifestation principles and practices to see which ones will work best for you. To manifest more easily, remember that these tools are *meant to be fun.* While I strive to present them in ways that are sensitive to trauma recovery, always check in with your own internal guidance and focus on the tools you enjoy. As you'll learn, the energy of fun and flowing with the Universe is something we want to tap into when manifesting. I want you to start trying these practices before you get into healing work because I believe that you don't have to be fully healed to start experimenting with tools to create your reality. I also want to make sure you know what I mean when I use the word "manifesting." Let's begin by looking at the most common explanations for how manifesting works.

Quantum explanations for manifesting have been popular for decades. They are based on theories related to quantum physics, consciousness, and metaphysics. They are the most common explanations and can be exciting theories to explore. If you like ideas that play with concepts of time, space, and energy, there are endless rabbit holes to go down. There are, however, pitfalls to be aware of when it comes to mental health.

A Quantum Warning

Quantum explanations for manifesting are vast, but they all come down to the idea that everything is made up of energy and that there is a quantum field of probability we can learn to tap into where anything is possible. If you believe in a quantum explanation of manifesting, you also believe that what you want to manifest exists somewhere in time or space. These explanations are the most controversial—some are based on research studies, and some are purely theoretical—and debated among the explanations for manifesting.

Whether you decide to believe is up to no one else but you. I am not a physicist. Quantum physics is undeniably complex. And yet, manifestation teachers and coaches will tell you they have *studied* quantum physics and can use it to explain exactly how manifesting works. What they typically mean by "studied," however, is that they watched a documentary, listened to a podcast, or read a book about the topic. This is not the same as being a physicist. Any doctoral degree takes years of arduous research, leads to nuance, and is humbling as it brings more questions than answers. I'm telling you this because coaches can make any claims they want about their expertise and charge you thousands of dollars for very little value. The quantum world can be enticing, but you'll want to enter with your eyes (not wallet) wide open.

The dilemma is that while exploring these explanations can be fun, doing so can trigger or exacerbate mental health symptoms. In my private practice, many clients report that learning about the Law of Attraction was harmful because it increased their level of anxiety or self-blame. You may have experienced this also. This is why I don't recommend focusing on quantum explanations in trauma-informed manifesting, and I encourage a healthy dose of skepticism. That said, there are fun quantum techniques that are less likely to increase anxiety, which I will soon share.

The Psychological Explanation

The psychological explanation for manifesting encompasses both psychology and neuroscience. From this perspective, we have beliefs based on experiences from our past that create neural pathways that unconsciously govern our nervous system, thoughts, emotions, and behaviors. These beliefs influence our reality and create the conditions of our lives. The neuroscientific explanation for manifestation also involves a bundle of nerves in your brain stem called the reticular activating system (RAS). The RAS filters information around us depending on what we think is important and what will help us survive. It involves *selective attention* (for example, I notice more Range Rovers when I want to manifest a Range Rover) and *confirmation bias* (for example, "I believe that I can't have a healthy relationship, and my RAS looks for evidence that confirms this belief all day long"). In this book, we'll work with this explanation by learning how to release emotional blocks and create new neural pathways in the chapters ahead. Some of the exercises in this chapter will give your RAS instructions so it attends to your goals in a helpful way.

The Spiritual Explanation

The spiritual explanation for manifesting is that we co-create our reality with a supportive Universe (or whatever name you prefer for a Higher Power) through the power of intention and surrender. The spiritual side of manifesting is composed of three equally important steps: asking, surrendering or letting go, and receiving. The strategies for each of the three steps encourage the opposite of pushing or striving for something—they prompt us to *allow* the Universe to intervene and assist us. In following these steps, the energy you're aiming for is "allowing" rather than "pushing." The proverbial saying "Don't push the river, it flows by itself" is a good reminder that it's unnecessary (and often counterproductive) to try to use force with the Universe. This chapter will give you tools to tap into the spiritual side of manifesting.

However, as the following table shows, "allowing" is easier said than done. This is especially true for someone with a history of trauma since it can increase fear of uncertainty and decrease the ability to trust. After all, there's a protective part of all of us that doesn't want to "allow" anything harmful. That's completely understandable after trauma. The word "allowing" may even feel triggering for you. If it is, try replacing it with different words, such as "flowing" or "ease."

Allowing Energy	Pushing Energy
Emotionally regulated	Emotionally dysregulated
Feels safe	Feels unsafe
Trusts	Doesn't trust
Believes in possibilities	Wrestles with doubt and disbelief
Creative and curious	Focused on survival
Energy is expansive	Energy is contracted
Present	Focused on future fears
Fun and playful	Serious
Process-focused	Outcome-focused
Sense of abundance	Sense of scarcity
Open to multiple solutions	Tunnel vision on one solution
Takes wise and inspired action	Action is based on fear and often excessive
Grows and learns from experience	Can't tolerate imperfect results
Can tolerate uncertainty	Has a very low tolerance for uncertainty
Able to connect and receive help	Tries to control and micromanage
Collaborative (wants everyone to win/thrive)	Competitive

Allowing Energy	Pushing Energy
Manifesting feels magical at times	Manifesting feels like very serious work
Able to let the Universe do some of the work	Unable to relinquish control
Doesn't like divine timing, but trusts it	Does not trust or accept divine timing
Gives the Universe time to line things up	Expects immediate results
Experiments with manifestation tools	Tries to follow manifestation rules rigidly
Feels secure regardless of results	Uses achievement to prove worthiness
Flows and manages obstacles well	Paddles upstream and resents obstacles
Is open to the best outcome	Tries to force a very specific outcome
Has reasonable performance goals	Expectations are excessively unrealistic
Uses manifesting to expand consciousness	Sees manifesting as a means to an end

Keep in mind that small, intermittent moments of allowing are enough. Intentionally set the bar low for yourself when you start your trauma-informed manifestation journey. Doing so will give you a chance to build your confidence and ability to trust slowly without needless pressure and frustration.

Be sure to give yourself compassion when your energy is more pushing than allowing; it will happen often, and that's okay. In later chapters, you'll learn tools to experience the energy of allowing more of the time.

Clarifying Your Intentions

Asking the Universe to help you manifest your desires begins with exploring your intentions. Intentions give our lives direction, and they are the motivation behind our goals. Consider:

- What do you want to manifest and why?

- Will the things you desire help you thrive?

- Are they a match for who you authentically are?

- Are they an expression of your best self?

- Or do they represent the things you don't actually like, but unconsciously yearn for in order to feel safe? For example, you might desire a career that is considered prestigious because you want to feel respected, but you don't actually enjoy doing the day-to-day work involved.

The intentions behind your goals come from either your wounds or your values. *Wound-based goals* come from unmet needs from childhood and toxic cultural messages. It's okay to want things you didn't receive in childhood. And it's understandable if you've absorbed what author Jennifer Wallace calls "toxic achievement culture"—the pressure to optimize performance because society tells us that our value comes from accomplishments.[19] But it's important to reflect on whether our goals line up with our actual values. The main difference between value-based goals and wound-based goals is that wound-based goals aren't fulfilling. They can make you look like you're living your best life on social media or make you think you'll get to live your best life once you achieve them. You may then experience the depression that can come with attaining wound-based goals. The paradox of achievement is that it can make life suddenly feel directionless or purposeless—until you have a new wound-based goal.

For example, Riley grew up without a lot of financial resources and dreamed of having an extravagant wedding one day. She used manifestation techniques to envision her dream and make it a reality very quickly. The wedding was grand, and Riley looked beautiful in her photos on social media. The only problem was that her marriage wasn't a match for her deepest desires in life. After a few months, her initially charming husband, whom she knew for only a year before the engagement, was not interested in the things that mattered most to her. He was ambivalent about having children, disliked traveling, and spent all his free time binge-watching shows. Despite getting the wedding she envisioned, Riley wasn't intentional about the type of relationship that might have aligned with her values: family, travel, and adventure. She achieved her wound-based goal but felt disappointed and directionless.

Value-based goals, on the other hand, come from what's authentic and meaningful to you; they help you thrive and experience emotional well-being. Acceptance and commitment therapy (ACT) research demonstrates that accepting emotions and taking action on values significantly improves mental health, quality of life, and even achievement. Your values are the things you choose to care about and commit to. Value-based goals help you live your best life now because even the process feels authentic and meaningful.

Discovering Your Valued Desires

When you state a clear and powerful intention to manifest something, you set in motion a chain of events. This activity will help you be sure that it is something you want to devote energy to.

1. Write down what you want to manifest. Be sure to state what you want rather than getting rid of something you don't want.

2. Write down your top five values in this area of your life. Ask yourself: "What do I care about in this area?" For example, you might want to manifest a new job, and your career values might be teamwork, innovation, challenge, fun, and respect.

3. Ask yourself: "Is what I want to manifest based on a wound or my values?" For example, are you trying to manifest a new job to impress others or because you want a job that lines up with your values?

4. If it's based on a wound, can you ask for something that is even better? Something that reflects how you want to live your life and thrive?

5. Consider the essence of what you want to manifest or what function it will serve. For example, if you want to manifest a house, you might want ample space for entertaining and a relaxing view. What qualities will it give you (peace, love, freedom, self-respect, liveliness)? Take your time thinking about the essence of what you want because, if you only focus on surface features, you might find that what you manifest doesn't serve your needs. For example, wanting a new job may represent the desire for pleasant company and a lively environment. If you don't know the essence of what you want, you might end up finding a new job that pays more but has a toxic work culture.

6. Write your (perhaps new) goal clearly and in the present tense. For example, you might state: *I now manifest (or have) a beautiful house in the country where I enjoy peace, nature, and spaciousness daily.*

Once you have clarified your intentions and have a goal identified, you can experiment with some manifesting techniques. There is a common myth that we need to be fully "healed" to get out there and start manifesting the things we want in life. A trauma-informed perspective is more encouraging: You don't need to be fully healed to start visualizing and taking inspired action. While there might be benefit to taking a break as you figure out an unhealthy pattern, healing is a long-term process, and it can be accelerated when you are in healthy relationships and environments.

But before trying any manifestation techniques, it's important to learn how to assess whether you are in the right state to do them. These techniques are powerful and fun when you're in what I call a *manifesting mood*, and ineffective and frustrating when you aren't.

When and How to Practice Manifestation Techniques

A *manifesting mood* is the optimal state for connecting to your dreams. It's when you feel centered and emotionally regulated. It's a lot easier to experience "allowing" energy rather than "pushing" energy and to feel aligned with your goals in this state. This is when you'll want to engage in manifestation practices. Here are some tips for assessing your state.

Don't engage with goals or manifesting when you are in a dysregulated state. For example, you'll want to avoid manifestation practices when you feel hungry, angry, lonely, or tired. The acronym HALT can help you remember that you are not in a manifesting mood and can try the practices at another time. (You'll learn all about manifesting moods in chapter 9.)

Also avoid the practices when you feel emotionally dysregulated: triggered, anxious, shutdown or dissociated, overwhelmed, and so forth. Rather than engaging in manifestation practices, attend to your physical and emotional needs. You can use the tools in chapter 3 to regulate your nervous system and come back to the manifestation practices another time. For now, get in the habit of asking yourself, "Am I in a manifesting mood?" before focusing on goals and manifesting.

One way to elevate your mood and make the manifestation practices feel more powerful is to take them to the level of communing with the Universe. Rather than mere mental exercises, see your practices as an invitation to the Universe to co-create the "heaven on earth" experience of thriving with you.

Because we tend to attribute credit elsewhere, keep a journal of your goals and practices. Check off successfully achieved goals and take notes on which practices work for you. You might want to start with smaller goals because it will take time to believe it is your manifestation efforts that are truly accomplishing them. Try the following practices *when you're in a manifesting mood* and see which ones you enjoy the most. Since the first one is a visualization practice, I invite you to read it first before trying it.

Visualizing Your Desired Outcome

Once you have a clear sense of what you want to manifest and the essence of it, using your imagination to visualize can help you get in the energetic space of having it. This activity will help you emotionally embrace your future reality. Keep in mind that it is less wishful thinking and more about creating a realistic "memory" of something that has already happened. Creating a "memory" has two potential benefits. The more real the visualization is to your unconscious mind, the more believable it will be and the less resistance you'll have to it. The other potential benefit involves a quantum understanding of manifesting. If you believe we live in a multiverse and there is no such thing as time, then by choosing this memory, you're jumping into the timeline in which it exists.

1. Close your eyes. (Trauma-informed modification: If closing your eyes feels uncomfortable or distressing, try imagining the visualization in your "mind's eye" with your eyes open.)

2. Start by visualizing the goal as if it's already achieved. If you want to manifest a house, imagine waking up in the morning in a home that's perfect for you.

3. To make it realistic to your brain, include things you already do. If it's a new home, imagine yourself eating your usual breakfast there, watching your favorite show there, petting your dog there, and so on.

4. To make it seem like a real memory to your brain, include vivid sensory details, especially smell because it is deeply connected to memory. For example, feel the cool touch of the fridge, the smell of your coffee, the warmth of the sun on the patio, and so forth.

5. Be sure to include how you will feel in the scenario (excited, joyful, peaceful) and savor this feeling for a few seconds. (Don't skip this important step.)

6. Don't try to figure out or visualize "how" you will manifest your goal. Just focus on your desired outcome.

7. Make the visualization like virtual reality and imagine moving around in the scene.

8. After a few minutes of visualizing the outcome, "bathe" in the essence or quality of your desire for a few seconds. For example, if you visualized a new romantic partner, bathe in the energy of love. Imagine the energy of love floating all around you.

9. End your visualization practice by setting the intention to be alert to the right opportunities and to have the ability to take action toward your desire.

You can listen to a recording of this visualization practice on the website for this book, http://www.newharbinger.com/53042.

Scripting Your Desired Outcome

Scripting is a manifestation practice that involves writing about a goal as if you've already achieved it. It's like writing a journal entry from the perspective of your future self. You can download a worksheet for this activity on the website for this book, http://www.newharbinger.com /53042.

1. Get your journal and a pen. Start with a prompt. Try one of the following:

    Today was a great day!

    Today, I celebrated because…

    Yesterday, I reached my goal!

2. Write about the goal as if it's a memory that has already happened.

3. Include how you felt and savor the feeling in your body for a few seconds.

4. To make it real, add details about what you already do in life (such as starting your day with coffee or a walk).

5. Include sensory details (how things looked, sounded, felt, and smelled).

6. Fill at least half a page.

A New Way to Vision Board

Vision boards are a visual depiction of your dreams. They usually include magazine cutouts, photos, and words that represent what you are working on manifesting. If you bring some playful and creative energy to it, a vision board can be powerful and fun. You can use paper, a posterboard, a notebook, or your computer to make a vison board. My one modification is to keep the vision board out of sight and only work on it or look at it when you are in a manifesting mood. This will help your brain associate your dreams with expansive emotions and make them feel more real and achievable. (You'll learn more about this in chapter 9.)

Learning to Trust

Manifesting with the Universe's help is a dance of co-creation. Sometimes you tell the Universe, "I got this," and you courageously take a step toward living your best life. Sometimes the Universe says, "Rest, I've got you," and you allow yourself to be held and taken care of while the Universe lines up the perfect opportunities.

In *The Power of Surrender*, Dr. Judith Orloff states: "Surrender doesn't mean being passive or impotent. It means leaving no stone unturned in manifesting your goals or solving a dilemma—but not letting the death grip of overefforting or being too obsessive sabotage you or stop magic from intervening."[20] This perfectly describes how co-creating requires a fine balance between effort and letting go.

Sometimes this important aspect of manifesting is called the Law of Detachment. Trying too hard out of a sense of desperation and urgency usually sabotages our intentions by repelling new ideas and straining new relationships. Trying to control and micromanage exactly how our goal manifests or getting attached to a specific outcome can also block what is right for us. If we believe in a supportive Universe, we might also consider that it evaluates our ability to thrive in the manifestation or situation we want and tries to steer us to the highest possibility. Rather than getting attached and clinging to a very specific outcome, we can *use it as a symbol of what we want* and make ourselves emotionally available for the best outcome. Sometimes the person, option, or solution we cling to as "the one" needs to be released so the best manifestation can come through.

There is an elegance to how the Universe responds when we let go. Once we trust that something even better is just around the corner, it orchestrates magical synchronicities and exciting opportunities that are a perfect fit for who we are. I see this happen time and time again for both my more intuitive and spiritual clients, as well as my very linear and logical ones. It doesn't matter if you believe in a spiritual version of manifesting that includes a Higher Power; it just matters that you release pushing for a little while.

I don't want to make light of how difficult this can be when we've experienced trauma. Control is how we feel safe. In the coming chapters, you'll work on healing so it gets easier to feel safe. For now, here are some tips for releasing your attachment to outcomes so that, rather than pushing and clinging, you can experience the peace of letting go:

- Ask for more. Rather than imagining having one job offer, imagine having three great offers to choose from. If you want to have a baby, imagine taking care of a baby and a toddler (or two babies!). Our minds love to solve problems, and if you're trying to manifest one viable option, the mind assumes that option is hard. If you give it the problem of having to manage multiple good options and manifestations, the sense of what's possible will expand. Instead of being fear-oriented, your mind will become opportunity-oriented and come up with new creative solutions.

- Keep all options on the table. Don't "fall in love" with one option and eliminate other options prematurely because that can trigger a scarcity mindset, increase anxiety, and lead to impulsive actions and an unhealthy preoccupation with things you don't have. While we want certainty, we often try to manufacture it prematurely by idealizing something and deciding that this one thing is "the one." Stay open.

- Turn the Rumi quote "What you seek is seeking you" into a mantra that you repeat to yourself. It can be a reminder that the Universe puts value-based desires in your heart because they are meant for you and are seeking you out as well.

- After doing a manifestation practice, repeat the affirmation from the classic manifestation book *Creative Visualization* by Shakti Gawain: "This, or something better, now manifests for me in totally satisfying and harmonious ways, for the highest good of all concerned."[21]

- Soothe the part of you that gets attached to outcomes. It is usually a wounded, scared younger part that's triggered. Have compassion for it and work on being the wise parent it needs rather than letting it take over. We'll cover how to reparent in depth in later chapters. For now, just recognize that when a younger part of you is anxious about how things will turn out, you can acknowledge and soothe their feelings.

- Have a centering practice.

Centering Practice

It's important to cultivate a regular centering practice so you can experience the *felt sense* of "dropping the rope" and letting go. Rather than pushing or playing tug-of-war with the Universe, you're co-creating and allowing. The practice should regulate your nervous system (you'll learn more about that in the coming chapters). It should also be efficient since short but regular practices are the most effective for rewiring your brain. Here are a few options for now:

- Put your hand on your heart and take a few deep breaths.

- Imagine light coming down through the top of your head and filling your whole body.

- Inhale for a count of 4 and exhale for a count of 8 (repeat two to four times).

Turning It Over to the Universe

This practice is a prayer you can use when you feel frustrated, desperate, and overwhelmed by your goal. It's simple but powerful enough to create what seem like miracles. It's the ultimate surrender. Recite the prayer with the intention to ask the Universe for assistance and to recognize and accept the help when it is offered.

I am turning this whole frustrating situation over to you, Universe. Please show me the way, or (kindly and gently) manifest it (or something better) for me. Thank you.

Learning to Receive

After you set your intentions and engage in manifestation practices, you'll start to receive guidance in two forms: inner guidance and outer guidance. Inner guidance looks like intuitive nudges or inspired thoughts. Outer guidance includes signs from the Universe and synchronicities, which are meaningful coincidences. Having a regular centering practice will help you be still and hear the inner guidance. Being more present while going about your day will help you notice outer guidance.

If you have an inspired thought or intuitive urge, follow it because it could lead you to your desired outcome. (Obviously, use good judgment here and don't do something dangerous.) You'll know it's an inspired thought because it will come out of nowhere and be different from your usual thoughts. For example, you suddenly have an urge to go to a different grocery store than usual. By following the nudge, you're taking *inspired action*. You could meet your future partner at that store or run into someone you've been thinking about—a synchronicity—who recommends a supplement that's on sale only today—a sign—that successfully heals your ailment.

Signs and synchronicities are like winks from the Universe. They are the way the Universe sends messages to us. Listening to your intuitive nudges and looking for signs and synchronicities can add a little magic to your day and help you develop trust.

Treasure Hunt

What you choose to look for is what you're going to see. In other words, the world often reflects our expectations. Try this activity to see how your reticular activating system (the part of the brain that selects what to focus on) works.

For the next few days, set the intention to look for and find the following objects and then actively search for them (one at a time). Take notes in your journal on what you observed including how many times you see it or anything unusual or unique about the circumstances.

1. Cars that are a shade of orange

2. Butterflies

3. Rainbows

After doing a treasure hunt for these objects, think about how your expectations can influence what you see. Can you do a treasure hunt for things that support what you're trying to manifest? Things that show you it is possible? For example, can you look for signs that the Universe is supporting your goal? This might show up as someone suggesting you pursue it, someone offering to help, or an answer spontaneously coming to you. After all, when we look for magic, we often find it.

Say Yes to the Universe

Even after the Universe delivers nudges, signs, and synchronicities, it will be up to you to accept them and any gifts the Universe offers. While you'll work on releasing blocks to self-worth and receiving gifts throughout the book, what I'm proposing involves opening up to the idea that, even after trauma, there is still good in the world and plenty of it is just for you.

Let me give you a quick example of a mini-manifestation with a big impact. Many years ago, I saw a pair of earrings I absolutely loved and wanted to buy, but I hesitated because I didn't want to splurge on myself. I decided not to buy them and left the store. Later that day, I found money on the ground outside that was the *exact* amount of the earrings. I waited around for a while to see if anyone was looking for the lost money, but the place was deserted. I went back to the store and bought the earrings that became my favorite for years to come. Every time I put them on, I was reminded that it's okay to receive and to say *yes* to the gifts the Universe gives us.

Saying *yes* to the Universe is saying *yes* to yourself.

Ask for what you want and try to appreciate what you receive. You don't have to turn it into an obligatory gratitude practice, just an occasional heartfelt recognition that the Universe heard you. This type of acknowledgment keeps the lines of communication clear and open.

Now that you have some manifestation techniques to play with, in the next chapter, we'll look at ways to regulate your nervous system so it's able to support your manifestation work and is better equipped to receive your desires.

Take-Home Points

- Evaluate your goals and aim for value-based ones that can help you thrive.

- Treat manifestation practices not as wishful thinking but as creating a memory of something that has already happened.

- Only engage in manifestation practices or focus on goals when you are in what I call a *manifesting mood*.

- Rather than getting attached and clinging to a very specific outcome, use your goal as a symbol of what you want and make yourself emotionally available for the best outcome.

- Allow the Universe to meet you halfway.

CHAPTER 3

Befriend Your Nervous System for Successful Manifesting

Polyvagal Theory is the science of feeling safe enough to fall in love with life and take the risks of living.

—Deb Dana, *Anchored*

Jada came to therapy because she felt stuck. She was an amateur baker who dreamed of opening an online cake shop that catered to people with food allergies. Despite winning a local award for her mouthwatering gluten-free petit fours, she wasn't making much progress. Rather than experimenting with plant-based paints and unique ingredients, she spent most of her time watching baking shows. Her friends were impressed with her whimsical designs and requested her signature vegan cupcakes for parties. But when party guests inquired about her services, Jada joked about not being a real pastry chef and quickly changed the topic. Instead of sharing content on her own baking social media account, she spent time looking at the accounts of bakers with massive followings. When I asked her what steps she was taking toward her business goals, she said that she recited positive affirmations regularly and visualized being a celebrity baker who shows the world that cakes without harmful ingredients can be delicious works of art.

Like Jada, you may also feel like your big dream isn't moving forward despite all of your hopes and best intentions. You might want to take the necessary practical steps, but without strategies to manage your stress response, you're at the mercy of your nervous system. It's your nervous system's job to protect you at all costs, including the cost of reaching your goals. Jada wasn't lazy or unmotivated. She grew up with narcissistic parents who would either criticize her mistakes or claim her achievements as their own. This made moving toward her goals feel dangerous. Her nervous system was doing its job by keeping her at a safe distance from being scrutinized or successful.

Before Jada could manifest her dreams, she needed to gain a sense of her past, reduce shame around nervous system dysregulation, learn regulation strategies to feel safe enough to take action, and practice manifestation techniques that her nervous system was ready for (such as visualizing setting up a simple website rather than being a world-famous baker). In other words, she first needed to learn to regulate her mind and body.

The biggest misconception about pursuing goals is that it is done primarily through willpower and self-control. When you believe this misconception, you are more prone to shame and further from sustainably achieving your goals. The truth is that pursuing your goals requires the ability to self-regulate. Self-regulation is the ability to manage your nervous system in the face of stress so you can behave in goal-directed ways to achieve your desired outcomes.

The ability to self-regulate impacts your thoughts, emotions, and behaviors as you pursue goals. Self-regulation helps you manage your mood, remain flexible and adaptable, persist despite challenges, and put forth your best effort. Sounds pretty good, doesn't it? But how can you do this when you have a history of trauma?

Trauma Compromises the Ability to Regulate

If your stress load is high because of trauma, especially long-term trauma, then you likely struggle to recover from stress. Your reactivity to stressors, even relatively minor ones, becomes heightened. This is why the popular manifestation advice to just forget the past doesn't work. For you, *the past gets involuntarily triggered in your nervous system in the present.* The result is one of the most common symptoms of trauma, especially complex trauma: chronic nervous system dysregulation. Dysregulation is a sustained stress response—which is a reaction to a perceived threat. When you struggle with chronic nervous system dysregulation, you are quick to react to anything you perceive as threatening (even if it is actually safe) and have a hard time coming back to feeling safe.

Dr. Stephen Porges's polyvagal theory provides a map of the autonomic nervous system and offers a new way of thinking about trauma and stress adaptation. According to this theory, your body is constantly scanning the environment for signs of safety, danger, and life threat in a process known as *neuroception*.[22] In order to keep you safe, your nervous system generalizes reminders of past painful experiences. This means that if you had traumatic experiences, you can continue to perceive cues of danger when none are present. This is called *faulty neuroception*. When your neuroception is faulty, you can detect risk where there is none and even detect safety where there is actual danger.

It's important to remember that neuroception is a process that is outside your awareness. A neuroception of danger from your body triggers an automatic survival response before you realize anything is happening. Because it's so fast and physiological, you can't just think your way out of getting triggered, and *you don't get to choose your survival response.* You jump or freeze when you see a snake-shaped stick *before* you consciously notice it and realize it's not a snake. And it isn't your fault.

As a result, you might get triggered often. If you don't have the skills to regulate your nervous system and feel safe, you can end up living in survival mode. You can have a hard time accessing your prefrontal cortex, which is the thinking part of your brain that helps you plan, communicate effectively, self-reflect, problem solve, and learn. Manifesting your goals in a dysregulated state like this isn't likely to work because it compromises your ability to think and communicate clearly. You're more likely to react to anything you perceive as an obstacle with a survival response. This can keep you from moving toward your goals, collaborating with people who could help you, and managing challenges along the way.

Before we learn some skills so dysregulation doesn't derail your goals, try this exercise to see which survival responses you identify with the most.

Stress Test

Imagine you are working on an important project that is due tomorrow when your computer suddenly stops cooperating. Maybe it doesn't completely crash, but it isn't doing what you want and clearly doesn't care about your deadline.

Imagine how you would feel in your body and pick a response that best captures your reaction:

A. **Fight stress response.** You can feel your blood boiling and energy running through your arms. You're annoyed and maybe even enraged. You start yelling obscenities at the computer. Maybe you look around to see if there's anyone else to blame. The cat who loves to stand right in front of the screen, the person who assigned the task or deadline in the first place, or maybe yourself for waiting until the last minute to start. No one is spared from the critical thoughts running through your head.

B. **Flight stress response.** *Oh no! Oh NO!* Sheer panic. You can feel your whole body mobilize to act. You start worrying about all the things that could go wrong if you don't meet your deadline. *What if? What if? What if?* Maybe you decide to go get some coffee while you try to figure out what to do next. As you're standing in front of the coffee machine, you look at your phone and start scrolling. Finally, there's some space between you and the problem! What problem?

C. **Freeze stress response.** You stare at the screen blankly. A few seconds go by, and you're still staring at the same fuzzy spot. The panic is overwhelming, and you feel stuck. Your thinking becomes foggy. Your body feels stiff, and you can barely move. *I need to fix this now! I can't! But I have to! Maybe I'll figure it out later.* You can't decide what you should do and end up missing the deadline.

D. **Fawn stress response.** *Oh no.* You don't want everyone to be mad at you! You don't even attempt to fix the issue because you have an overwhelming urge to reach out to someone. Maybe you should check on your boss to see what kind of mood they're in today in case this gets worse? Maybe you should call an IT person? Surely, they know more than you do. You call them immediately. You apologize for wasting their time, compliment them on their skills, and thank them for rescuing you before they even look at the problem.

To be fair, most of us have probably responded to a computer issue with all of the above at one point or another. We evolved to survive using these strategies for good reason. They're adaptive and actually brilliant when we are faced with real danger. Dysregulation is a problem when we don't know how to adjust the intensity of our stress response and reliably bring ourselves back to feelings of safety. When we're going on a date or giving a presentation, we need to be able to regulate our responses so they don't negatively impact our goals.

Your Autonomic Nervous System States

Jada, the hesitant baker, reacted to the stressors involved in starting her business with a freeze response. She felt overwhelmed and wasn't able to take the necessary steps to reach her goals. Her thoughts reflected this state: *I must, but I can't.* From a polyvagal theory perspective, she wasn't simply procrastinating; she was stuck because her autonomic nervous system was dysregulated, and she didn't have the skills yet to regulate it. Our autonomic nervous system is divided into three parts:

1. **Dorsal vagal system.** Sometimes called the dorsal vagal complex, this is your earliest system. Much like the emergency brake in your car, this system freezes and immobilizes you when you're faced with a threat and can't escape. Signs that this system is activated include feeling helpless, fatigue, lethargy, depression, dissociation, foggy thinking, procrastination, shutting down, and fainting. When this system is activated, your nervous system is *hypo*aroused, and you might feel numb and even physically cold.

2. **Sympathetic system.** Much like the gas pedal in your car, this system mobilizes you. It helps you fight or flee in the face of danger. You might feel anger, rage, anxiety, or restlessness when this system is activated. In this state, your nervous system is *hyper*aroused, and you might even feel physically flushed or hot.

3. **Ventral vagal system.** This is your most recent system. Sometimes it's called the ventral vagal complex or the social engagement system. It's like using a soft brake in your car when you see a nice beach you want to visit and decide to slow down and park. When this system is activated, you feel safe, connected, and present. In this state, you feel good, and your body is likely to feel "just right" as opposed to too cold or too hot.

While your autonomic nervous system is made up of two branches (sympathetic and parasympathetic), the vagus nerve in the parasympathetic branch has two pathways: dorsal and ventral. You may have heard about the vagus nerve in the last few years as improving vagal tone has grown in popularity. Improving vagal tone is essentially engaging in practices such as humming and ice baths in order to get better at nervous system regulation. Trauma results in an underactive ventral vagal system, which is why regular practices that promote ventral vagal energy are so important. Before taking up cold plunging, let's look at which strategies might be best for you depending on how you approach manifesting.

What Type of Manifestor Are You?

To help you understand how your nervous system could be impacting your efforts to manifest important goals and which strategies you should focus on, read the following manifestor types and see which one you identify with the most.

The daydreamer. Your imagination is your refuge. You are drawn to visualization, vision boards, and meditation. You have big dreams but can get overwhelmed by them. Your attachment style is on the avoidant side, and you believe that you need to do everything alone.

(You'll learn all about attachment styles in chapter 5.) The result is that no one knows when you're struggling. The truth is that it's hard for you to take action on your dreams. You tend to get stuck in a dorsal vagal state regularly and could benefit from ventral practices that help you accept support or assistance and take small action steps toward your goals regularly.

The hustler. You love to take action and can make progress quickly. You listen to motivational podcasts while working out and like to try different life hacks. You're always on the move, but sometimes your actions have negative consequences. Your attachment style is on the anxious side, and you tend to try to control situations rather than allow things to unfold. Sometimes you overprioritize achieving goals, leading to relationship problems, guilt, and adrenal fatigue. You spend a lot of time in a sympathetic state and have what's sometimes called "trauma drive"—motivation that's fueled by fear. You could benefit from ventral vagal practices that help you safely slow down, have more balance, and recover from stress.

The complex manifestor. You have both daydreamer and hustler tendencies, and at times, this feels confusing and intense. Your attachment style is on the disorganized side. Because you shift between sympathetic states and dorsal states quickly, your manifestation results are mixed. You chase your goals one minute and feel swallowed up by despair and inertia the next. Your thinking also depends on your state and can be extreme: one minute, you idealize things and see them as all good; the next, you devalue or villainize things and see them as all bad. This creates a push-pull dynamic that can make it hard to hold on to the things you manifest. You could benefit from ventral vagal practices that help you find safety in each state and allow you to start feeling stable and seeing things as both-and.

The self-healer. You engage in practices that help you increase vagal tone regularly, but you're not perfectionistic about them. You use your imagination to dream big and take action when it's needed. You like to take time to be alone so you can connect to your healing process. You seek out people who are good for your nervous system, and your approach to relationships is to "regulate before you communicate." You actively work on developing a secure attachment style. You trust yourself and are resilient. Your willingness to engage with healing, even if it is very slow, makes it easier for you to manifest the things you want in life because they are simply a reflection of who you have become.

If the self-healer type sounds a little too pie-in-the-sky for you right now, don't get discouraged. Many people with trauma will find themselves in one of the other categories when they start a healing journey. The self-healer type is the goal of this book regardless of where you are now. By practicing the skills, you're on your way to healing and transforming your life to match your dreams.

Regulation Skills

The nervous system regulation practice you should use depends on the state you are in. As you'll see, when you're in a sympathetic state, you'll want to use strategies to downregulate, and when you're in a dorsal state, you'll want to use strategies to upregulate. If you have a history of trauma, you might find that you flip-flop from sympathetic to dorsal and back again throughout the day. Use the strategy you need for your current state. Try to keep track of strategies that work for you so you can use them again. And remember, regulation strategies require practice. You don't wait until you're drowning to learn how to swim. A small amount of practice often is best.

Greet Dysregulation with Compassion and Curiosity

Regardless of whether you are using a strategy to downregulate or upregulate your nervous system, keep in mind that shame and self-criticism often accompany survival responses. Use the following practice I adapted from the well-researched work by Dr. Kristin Neff and Dr. Chris Germer on mindful self-compassion to help you move out of dysregulation and protection and into regulation and safety.[23]

The next time you feel triggered and dysregulated, take a moment to step out of the experience and be kind to yourself. Notice that you are triggered and say the following phrases to yourself:

1.   I feel dysregulated.

2.   Dysregulation is a part of life.

3.   May I be kind to myself during dysregulation.

Feel free to change the words to see what resonates with you. The purpose of the exercise is to bring awareness and self-compassion to moments of distress. This is how you start to befriend your nervous system. The exercises that follow will give you more practical ideas for bringing ventral vagal energy (feelings of safety) to moments of dysregulation.

Grounding

Grounding is an essential skill for doing any healing work. It refers to being present in your body in this moment. When you feel dysregulated and ungrounded, you can start to panic or dissociate. Practice this exercise regularly so it becomes a skill you can easily access when you really need it.

1.   Sit in a chair and notice the feeling of your feet on the ground.

2.   Wiggle your toes and press your feet against the ground.

3.   Move your head (not just your eyes) to look around the room and name five things you see.

4.   Name four things you hear. Maybe it's an air conditioner, a radio, a bird, or a lawn mower.

5.   Name three things you feel. Maybe it's your soft sweater, your cool water bottle, or the ground beneath your feet.

6.   You can continue to get back into your senses by naming things you smell or taste.

Practices to Downregulate from Sympathetic
Prolonged Exhale

The autonomic nervous system is affected by breathing speed. Rapid breaths and incomplete exhales signal sympathetic states, while incomplete inhales signal a dorsal state. Studies show that prolonged exhales stimulate our vagus nerve and signal to our nervous system that we are safe.[24] This breathing exercise is designed to help you downregulate from an activated sympathetic state. Try it out during moments of stress.

1. Inhale through your nose for a count of 4. Makes sure it's a deep breath that fills up your diaphragm.

2. Exhale through your mouth for a count of 8. Make sure it's a complete exhale.

3. If you can, drop your shoulders and release tension from your body during the exhales.

4. Repeat about four times.

Cold

The autonomic nervous system is affected by temperature. To downregulate from a sympathetic state, try using different methods involving cold. When you are stressed, try these strategies to cool off your nervous system:

- Splash cold water on your face.

- Hold ice cubes or a cold bottle of water in your hands.

- Put a cold compress on your forehead or the back of your neck.

- Drink icy cold water.

- Get some cool, fresh air.

Movement

Sympathetic states have the energy to mobilize you, which means that intentionally moving the energy through your body can be regulating. These movements can be smaller when appropriate (like using fidgets at school or work) or much bigger (like full-body movements, such as running or dancing). Experiment with different physical activities that safely discharge sympathetic energy to see which ones work best for you.

Clean or Declutter

Cleaning can be a productive way to discharge sympathetic energy and to feel organized inside and out. Pick one room or one drawer and start cleaning.

Sing or Hum

Singing and humming stimulate the vagus nerve and help you feel regulated.

Co-Regulate

Mirror neurons in our brains allow us to have strong empathy for others. They also give us the ability to be influenced by someone else's regulated state. To practice this skill, think about the people and pets you know who tend to be well regulated and have a lot of ventral vagal energy. The next time you feel stressed, try one of these strategies:

- Call a supportive friend and ask them to hold space for you (to listen without trying to fix things).

- Snuggle your pet or visit an animal shelter.

- Walk your dog or use an app to become a casual dog walker (you'll get plenty of friendly co-regulating smiles from fellow dog lovers when you walk a dog).

- Schedule a therapy appointment if possible.

Practices to Upregulate from Dorsal

Imagined Movement

When you're in a dorsal state, movement needs to be slow and gentle so you don't accidentally jolt yourself into a sympathetic state. If it is particularly difficult to move when you're in a dorsal state, try imagining moving in ways that are pleasing to you. For example, you can sit on the couch, but imagine ice-skating or walking on a beach. Play with this exercise to see what works best for you.

Sit on an Exercise Ball

If you feel ready for gentle movements, try sitting on an exercise ball. The small, ongoing movements can keep you from moving further down into dorsal.

Use a Rocking Chair

There's a reason rocking chairs and gliders are popular among new parents. Babies are soothed by gentle rocking movements and, as it turns out, so are adults. If this feels like a good fit for you, consider buying a rocking chair, glider, or swing.

Gentle Walk

If it feels regulating to do so, go on a gentle walk. This is a great way to ground yourself and possibly co-regulate if you're with a dog, a supportive person, or in nature (many people find nature to be supportive).

Use Warmth

Warmth is an intuitive way to thaw a freeze response. Here are a few ways to move out of dorsal using temperature.

- Drink a cup of hot tea.

- Take a warm bath or shower.

- Put on a warm sweater.

- Snuggle under blankets (some people like to use weighted blankets).

Prayer or Meditation

Prayer and meditation can connect us to a physical and emotional sense of safety. If this is the case for you, take a moment to say a prayer or meditate when your energy level starts to dip into dorsal. Just keep in mind that not all meditations are trauma-sensitive, and that it is perfectly okay to opt out (and ground yourself) if you feel triggered by any meditation exercise.

Co-Regulate

Moving out of a dorsal state through connecting with others can be extremely effective. And yet, when you're in a dorsal state, it can be exceptionally difficult to express yourself verbally. Often, it's best to seek out people who are understanding and will either just be present with you or allow you to communicate at your own speed. Here are a few gentle ideas to move out of dorsal and toward connection:

- Start by imagining being around someone who is supportive.

- Go to a cafe or bookstore where there are other people, but you don't have to interact.

- Watch a movie or take a walk with a friend or family member.

- Text or call someone who is supportive.

- Pet an animal.

- Schedule a therapy appointment if possible.

Make a List of Your Ventral Vagal Resources

We all have things that can reliably give us moments of safety. Using your journal, make a list of the people, pets, spiritual figures, places, activities, things, and somatic resources that give you a glimpse of safety. You can download a worksheet for this activity on the website for this book, http://www.newharbinger.com/53042. Here's an example of what your list might look like:

People, Pets, or Spiritual or Religious Figures (Pick Ones That Feel Safe and Regulating)

1. *My dog*

2. *My cousin, because she's a great listener*

3. *My spirit guide*

Places

1. *The beach*

2. *The bookstore or coffee shop*

3. *Nature trails*

Activities

1. *Walking*

2. *Reading*

3. *Drawing*

Things

1. *My favorite shows*

2. *Crystals*

3. *Tea*

Somatic Resources

1. *Deep breathing*

2. *Giving myself a hug*

3. *Putting my hand on my heart*

Get creative and combine regulating activities if you find it helpful. For example, you can take a walk while listening to an uplifting podcast. Or you can sip warm tea and snuggle under warm blankets. The combinations are endless, and the strategies listed here are not exhaustive by any means.

The important thing is to take regulation seriously. It's not selfish to take care of your nervous system. At the same time, don't feel guilty if you're not sticking to regular regulation activities. If you find yourself avoiding one activity, try another until you find the right fit for you. Just be intentional about choosing activities because they can help you upregulate or downregulate, depending on what your nervous system needs in the moment.

How Regulation Changes Your Thinking

Nervous system regulation doesn't just help you take productive steps toward your goals; it also changes your thinking. According to polyvagal theory, your thoughts are the result of your nervous system state. Therapist Deb Dana encapsulates this idea with the phrase "story follows state."[25] You can see which state you are in by looking at your thoughts. In a sympathetic state, your thoughts are anxious, catastrophizing, or aggressive. In a dorsal state, they are pessimistic, hopeless, helpless, and apathetic. In a ventral state, your thoughts are supportive, validating, hopeful, resourceful, and resilient.

Popular manifestation advice emphasizes the importance of positive thinking, which can stress us out. The mandate to think positively or else we'll never manifest what we want can easily dysregulate our nervous system and make positive thoughts inaccessible. But positive thinking isn't something you need to strive for. It's more important to focus on regulating your nervous system so you can enjoy the benefits of what I like to call *supportive thinking*. Supportive thinking comes naturally when you're in a ventral vagal state. Supportive thinking sounds like:

- *I've got this!*

- *I'll be okay no matter what.*

- *I totally get why this is hard for me, and I give myself compassion.*

- *I know I have the resources to deal with this.*

- *I know who to reach out to for help when I need it.*

- *It makes sense that I feel this way.*

- *I set boundaries because I care about myself too.*

- *I like taking care of myself.*

- *There are many ways for me to get what I need and want.*

- *I can do it.*

- *I did it!*

As you can see, nervous system regulation can help you think more "positive" thoughts without mental effort or added stress. And since feelings of helplessness increase stress, knowing that you can successfully practice regulation strategies can boost your confidence and decrease stress. Studies show that if you feel confident in your ability to manage stress, you'll actually feel less stressed.[26] In other words, befriending your nervous system is a powerful path to manifesting your goals with more optimism, resilience, and ease.

How Regulation Is Different from Avoidance

Nervous system regulation involves using voluntary strategies when we are involuntarily triggered. When you don't use these strategies, your dysregulation will escalate, or you'll unconsciously engage in activities to avoid the feelings that are triggered. Maybe it's self-soothing with food, pornography, substances, shopping, overexercising, or something else; one way or another, you'll find ways to manage dysregulation. The strategies in this chapter require conscious decision making. Therefore, they are healthy forms of active coping and healing.

Without regulation strategies, it would be difficult to engage with the feelings that are triggered when you have a neuroception of danger. Next, you'll learn trauma-informed strategies for sitting with your feelings and releasing stress and emotions from your body. These strategies can help you unblock the emotions that inevitably surface when you're pursuing your longed-for dreams.

Take-Home Points

- Understanding your nervous system helps reduce shame.

- Your autonomic nervous system is involuntary.

- Trauma can lead to chronic nervous system dysregulation.

- Your nervous system states impact your thoughts, feelings, and behaviors.

- The safer your nervous system feels, the more on board it will be with your goals.

- The more you practice nervous system regulation strategies, the easier it will be for you to successfully move in the direction of your dream life.

CHAPTER 4

Release Stress and Emotional Blocks to Goals

Every single time you relax and release, a piece of the pain leaves forever.

—Michael A. Singer, *The Untethered Soul*

I love to hear a great manifestation success story. Don't you? Stories of people who've used practices like visualization or a vision board to imagine the future they wanted and then lived it. I especially enjoy the ones that involve overcoming great odds. After reading this book, I want that for you too—I want you to have your own manifestation success story. But to get there, it's important to understand the role of releasing stuck emotions.

Our bodies tend to hold on to emotions when we're in a highly distressed state and can't successfully release the energy. For example, if you experienced a mugging and couldn't run away (or shake off the excess energy after the incident), the feeling of fear and the need to fight or flee will get "stuck." The stress response will be incomplete, and the sensations you experienced will feel "undigested." Your nervous system will act as if the trauma is ongoing, even years later. As a result, you might become hypervigilant—constantly on the lookout for danger—and ready to fight or flee even in safe situations. Stuck energy can put you in survival mode even when it's unnecessary. It's why trauma leaves you feeling chronically dysregulated.

What if you could permanently release some of the survival energy—stuck stress and trapped emotions from the past—from your body and no longer needed to constantly regulate? How would you pursue your goals if manifesting no longer had any survival energy attached to it?

If you want to manifest goals without survival-level fear, it's important to learn how to release stuck stress and emotions from the body. The more you release, the more confident and resilient you'll feel when it comes to pursuing the things that matter to you. Your nervous system will be regulated more of the time, and your thoughts will naturally be more supportive. You'll feel safer and go after your dreams with a relaxed assuredness. In other words, once you release trapped emotions, you'll be free to create new experiences!

If you're tempted to skip this chapter because the idea of releasing emotions is daunting, I hear you. I, too, ran from releasing deeply stuck emotions for a long time. Cut yourself some slack. Believe it or not, it's healthy to avoid releasing trauma-filled emotions unless it's done in a safe way. I've seen too many well-intentioned retreat leaders and coaches instruct people to go to their deepest traumas, just feel their feelings, and let them out. In this chapter, you'll learn why this approach can be harmful and learn gentler ways to release stuck emotions and stress. You'll discover that releasing doesn't have to involve cognitively revisiting your traumas; it can be done by working gently with activation in your body. This is the essence of bottom-up processing of stress arousal and emotions.

Before we continue, see if the following list of understandable fears are holding you back from exploring the possibility of releasing your emotions.

Emotional Release Avoidance Inventory

Which (legitimate) fears are stopping you from trying to release your emotions?

- Fear of losing control
- Fear of reliving your trauma

- Fear of being overwhelmed

- Fear of dissociating

- Fear of getting in touch with your bodily sensations

- Fear of having to talk about your trauma

- Fear that you'll remember your trauma

- Fear that you won't remember your trauma (and doubt whether it's legitimate)

- Fear of embarrassment (if other people are around)

- Fear that once you start feeling, you'll never stop

When we learn how to release emotions and stress in the body in a regulated way, many of these fears subside. Through gentle pacing, we can process and release emotions and stress arousal somatically without revisiting past traumas and without getting dysregulated. To start, let's look at how managing the intensity of emotions can help you avoid getting overwhelmed.

Titration: Managing the Intensity of Feelings

Somatic therapists (therapists who work primarily with the body) often define trauma as something that happens "too much, too soon, or too fast" for our nervous system to handle. This is why it's so important to slow things down when you're healing trauma. The process of slowly engaging with a small amount of trauma activation in the body at a time is called *titration*.[27]

In chemistry, titration refers to two different substances being mixed together one drop at a time in order to prevent an explosive reaction. Each drop will still cause a fizzle, but not an explosion. Gradually, the drops will accumulate and form a new substance. In the medical field, titration refers to taking a low dose of a drug in order to see how your body interacts with it; this limits potential side effects while finding an effective dose. In trauma healing, titration invites you to find your own pacing and give yourself room to feel and release stress and emotions in a regulated way so you don't get *emotionally flooded*—feel overwhelmed by an emotion and shut down. Rather than providing healing, the nervous system overwhelm that comes with emotional flooding can lead to retraumatization.

Titration is basically about not biting off more than you can chew. As you progress through this chapter, you will work with smaller, more tolerable amounts of stress activation or emotion at a time. You need to give yourself a chance to pause and digest. This is why, throughout your journey with this book, we will work with activation that is only slightly outside of your comfort zone. The emotions and sensations there might be uncomfortable, but not unbearable. You'll experience discomfort, but not distress. Working the edge of your comfort zone in this way is how you widen it.

Your Ability to Tolerate Emotions

Your *window of tolerance* (WOT) is the capacity of your nervous system to be present with emotions, sensations, and experiences without becoming overly activated or shutting down.[28] Essentially, when you are in your WOT, you feel regulated and safe. You are in your optimal zone of arousal.

When you are outside your WOT, you feel dysregulated and go into survival mode. Your prefrontal cortex goes offline and makes it difficult to access clear thinking and communication. Your rational brain becomes inaccessible, and your survival brain takes over. In this state, your thoughts are more likely to be negatively biased. This is why, when you're outside your WOT, it's important not to believe your thoughts, but to simply be aware that you're having distressed thoughts. The effect that dysregulation has on thinking is also why traditional manifestation teachings related to positive thinking tend to fall short when you're outside your WOT. These teachings advise you to always think positively so you attract positive outcomes, but it's nearly impossible to think positively in a dysregulated state. This is why it's better to focus on regulation rather than positive thinking.

The smaller your window, the more easily and often you get dysregulated. Unfortunately, trauma leads to a smaller WOT. Sleep, health issues, adverse life circumstances, and even judging emotions can also affect the size of your WOT. Anything that throws you into survival mode long enough can shrink your WOT. Fortunately, it's possible to expand it.

Understanding your WOT will help you expand it and give you back a sense of control and agency. You'll notice when you're stepping in and out of your window and recognize when it's time to use regulation strategies. You'll also discover that being in your WOT while trying to work with emotions and release them is important. For it to be healing, you need to be present and regulated enough to observe your emotions without getting overwhelmed by them. As you experiment with the exercises in this chapter, track your experience to make sure you're in your WOT or only slightly outside it. This is vital for self-regulation, and it's something you can learn to do with the information and practice I'll offer next.

Your Nervous System States and How They Feel

Let's get to know your WOT better. In the following chart, you'll find some common signs that dysregulation is starting to happen. The center column is your optimal zone. If you drift into either hyperarousal or hypoarousal, the following feelings can arise. Catching these signs *early* makes it infinitely easier to self-regulate. Rather than waiting until dysregulation is intense, you can spot these signs and use the strategies I'll soon share to return to your WOT much faster.

Nervous System States

Hyperarousal (Sympathetic) "Too hot"	WOT (Optimal Zone of Arousal) (Ventral Vagal) "Just right"	Hypoarousal (Dorsal Vagal) "Too cold"
Mobilized	Engaged	Immobilized
Increased heart rate	Normal heart rate	Slowed heart rate
Quick shallow breathing	Deeper rhythmic breathing	Slow shallow breathing
Hot, flushed	Comfortable temperature	Cold
Ungrounded	Grounded in body	Disconnected from body
Anxious, angry	Content	Depressed
Tense	Calm	Numb
Vigilant	Curious	Shutdown
Worried	Hopeful	Hopeless, helpless
Urge to move or act	Able to take action as needed	Inert, frozen
Racing thoughts, trouble focusing	Able to focus and process information	Foggy, spacey, unable to focus or process information
Reactive	Responsive	Withdrawn

Any time you feel like you're exiting your WOT, review the grounding and regulation techniques from chapter 3 and use them. For example, when someone mentions a stressful upcoming family function, you might notice a subtle increase in your heart rate. This is your cue to start using a regulation tool, such as prolonged exhales, to come back into your WOT. Noticing these signs requires the ability to sense what's happening inside of you, and it's a skill you can develop with a little practice.

Feel What's Happening Inside Your Body

Your capacity to "feel inside" or "see within" yourself and notice your internal states is called *interoception*. This type of awareness of how you feel physically and emotionally is important for releasing stress and emotions. Without it, it's hard to identify, regulate, or release emotions. And yet, trauma can make it uncomfortable to focus on what's happening internally. We disconnect because noticing sensations and emotions can be overwhelming and feel unsafe when we don't have regulation skills to manage them. It's understandable if you want to work on interoception in small doses and be gentle with yourself when you're just learning how to notice and regulate. To try it, take a moment and ask yourself:

- "What do I notice happening on the inside?"

- "Where do I feel the sensations I'm noticing in my body?"

- "Can I describe the sensations with words?"

The best way to develop interoception is to start noticing and naming your physical sensations. These can include things like hunger pangs, thirst, fatigue, lethargy, agitation, restlessness, sweating, feeling too hot or too cold, rapid or slow heartbeat, shallow breathing, comfort, discomfort, pain, or tension. Bringing your awareness to the information your body is making available to you is how you learn to identify whether you are inside or outside your WOT. Noticing your sensations can help you discern whether the level of activation in your body matches the level of threat in the present moment. By pausing to do this, you might recognize that you are safe right now and can focus on regulation rather than managing threats.

When you put your awareness on your physical sensations, you can also help areas that hold emotional pain release tension. To do this in a titrated way, so that it doesn't feel overwhelming, we will use a gentle technique called pendulation.

Gently Move Between Stress and Support

Imagine the pendulum of a clock swinging back and forth. Similarly, *pendulation* is switching your interoceptive awareness between comfort and discomfort in your body.[29] It can also be intentionally swinging between emotion regulation and dysregulation in order to safely release emotions, expand your WOT, and learn how to get back to a regulated state easily.

The first focal point in pendulation is an area of your body, or emotional state, that is activated, tense, or holding emotional distress. Choose something that is manageable so you can gently challenge and expand your WOT. For example, on a scale of one to ten, ten being highly distressing, you might choose a sensation or emotion that is around a three or four. While you'll only be sitting with this sensation or feeling very briefly, it should still be something tolerable. By doing this practice, you'll eventually expand your WOT so you can comfortably manage more intense sensations and feelings.

The second focal point is an area of your body that is grounded, stable, and supported. Often these areas are your feet, seat, or back. Take a moment and feel the place where your back or lower body meets the chair or where your feet touch the floor. See if this can give you the *felt sense*—or sensation-based feeling—of being supported and grounded. Trauma expert and developer of Somatic Experiencing Dr. Peter Levine calls these "islands of safety."[30] They make your body feel more like an ally in recovery. The more islands of safety you find and feel, the more you rewire a sense of stability in your body and emotions. (If you prefer, you can use a regulating resource from your ventral vagal resources list rather than an area of your body as your second focal point.)

Pendulation includes titration because you will slowly engage with small amounts of activation at a time. This can be accomplished by shifting attention between an upsetting emotion and a regulating resource. For example, you could focus on low-level anxiety for a few moments, then take a few deep calming breaths with long exhales (the resource in this case), then focus on the anxiety again, then take slow long exhales, and so on until you feel like the stress activation is being released. By doing so, you're healing through your body by showing it that it's possible to safely feel and release.

In the following exercise, you will learn what to do when you notice an emotion coming up or stress activation in your body. This exercise asks you to alternate focus between stress activation and support in order to relieve tension and release emotions in a regulated way. While sitting with feelings, stay mindful of your WOT and use techniques from the last chapter if you feel too dysregulated. You'll be moving in and slightly out of your WOT intentionally in order to expand it.

Moving Between Stress and Support[31]

This exercise is not about diving into traumatic memories or highly charged sensations in the body. Try to master using this activity with less distressing emotions before moving on to bigger ones. (You may need the assistance of a therapist to co-regulate while you do this with bigger emotions.) It's a gentle practice so you don't get overwhelmed and end up having no choice but to protect yourself from feelings. Instead, you can slowly gain agency over feelings of activation. For now, you're only gently and briefly sitting with discomfort.

1. When you are ready, place your awareness on a neutral or stable part of your body. It can be an area of your body that feels solid and grounded. It could be the place where your feet meet the ground or where your back meets the chair. If you prefer, use a regulating resource rather than a body location; perhaps it's slow deep breathing, a spiritual figure, nature, or a beloved pet. You can also use one of the ventral resources from your list in the previous chapter.

2. Spend a few minutes connecting to the stable part of your
    body or the resource you've chosen. What does it feel like? If
    it's a resource, what does it look like? What do you like about
    it? Allow yourself to sink into a soothing, comfortable con-
    nection to this body part or resource.

3. Next, release the comfortable experience and begin to notice
    if there is an uncomfortable emotion present or a part of your
    body that feels uncomfortable. (If at any time you become
    overwhelmed, remember to stop the practice and do a
    grounding exercise from chapter 3.)

4. In your mind's eye, see if the uncomfortable emotion or phys-
    ical sensation has a color, size, location, or shape to it. How
    might you describe it? Allow words to come to mind. Stay
    with this discomfort briefly (under a minute). Once you feel
    the discomfort rise, but still stay manageable, it's time to dis-
    engage from it and lower your distress level.

5. Let go of the discomfort you've been feeling, focus on the
    stable body part or resource, and allow it to comfort you. Stay
    with this feeling for as long as it feels good to do so.

6. Great job! You contracted with a *small taste* of dysregulation
    or discomfort and expanded with a moment of regulation.
    This natural rhythm of contraction and expansion will build
    your ability to sit with emotions and sensations longer
    without getting overwhelmed.

After practicing this movement between stress and support many
times, you may develop the ability to titrate your distress level by allowing
yourself to feel a little more discomfort or to feel discomfort for longer.
Over time, you'll have a higher tolerance for stress and become more
resilient—which will give you confidence in your ability to cope with
challenges during your manifestation journey.

Sitting with Feelings Longer

The chemicals associated with emotions run their course surprisingly fast—so fast that the biochemical lifespan of an emotion is approximately ninety seconds.[32] One way to think about it is that your emotions are like waves: they crest, peak, and fall. What goes up, must come down. If you can ride the wave of energy and temporary sensations, you can release the emotion. If you're wondering why this rarely feels true for you, consider three main reasons emotions can last longer than ninety seconds.

You fight emotions. You prolong the physiological experience of an emotion when you try to suppress or fight it. You usually fight an emotion if you've been taught that emotions are bad (as is the case with toxic positivity) or if you have a very valid fear of being flooded by an emotion because of past trauma. This is why titration is so important and why you need to work up to sitting with emotions for longer periods.

You create stories about emotions. The other way you might prolong the physiological experience of an emotion is when you create a story about the emotion. While emotions are messengers letting you know what's going on inside and what you need, you might not focus on the current message. Instead, you might get wrapped up in a story about the emotion based on the cascade of stress chemicals rushing through your body. If the emotion is sadness, it will be easier for your brain to pull up previous experiences of sadness that color your perception. Once you start thinking about the story and the old memories it triggered, you fire off more feelings. This is why it's important to create some distance by observing your emotions mindfully (you can find examples of how to do this in chapter 1). When you don't overidentify with an emotion, it's easier to resist the urge to create a story. If you do find that you're creating a story, you can state the following helpful line out loud: "I am telling myself the story that…" Hearing this out loud can help you see the story without believing it and playing it on repeat.

You can have multiple waves of emotions. We are complex, and it's not uncommon to experience multiple emotions simultaneously. For example, you can be excited to start a new project and anxious about all the work involved. Once they're activated, multiple waves of emotions will last over ninety seconds even if you're able to feel them fully and release them.

Keep in mind that sitting with an emotion requires presence. The goal is to observe the wave of an emotion in your body without reacting to it or creating a story about it. Then, when you remain regulated, you can approach it with curiosity and compassion. This is what we're working toward by increasing your WOT through pendulation with feelings of safety.

If you have a history of trauma, only attempt sitting with feelings for longer periods after you have worked on expanding your WOT for a while. Even if you are starting to master regulating your nervous system, you might still need the presence of a therapist to help co-regulate your feelings related to traumatic memories. Working with traumatic memories usually requires more intensive and structured treatments. Stay mindful of your WOT if you're considering sitting with your feelings and go back to grounding exercises whenever you feel overwhelmed.

You've probably heard about how mindfulness meditation is beneficial for mental health, including managing overwhelm. However, there's ample research showing mindfulness meditation can have adverse effects, especially for trauma survivors. Unfortunately, mindfulness practice, especially at retreats, can potentially be retraumatizing for trauma survivors because it encourages sitting with sensations and feelings for extended periods of time. According to one study, 58 percent of meditators reported at least one adverse meditation effect.[33] Some potential effects include flashbacks, dissociation, emotional blunting, depression, anxiety, disrupted sleep, nightmares, cognitive impairments, and social withdrawal.[34] If you are considering a retreat, look at options that include trauma-informed instructors. You can also track your level of distress and use tools for returning to your WOT. The more you understand trauma, the easier it is to reduce shame around dysregulation and to develop confidence in your ability to cope and heal.

While processing and releasing emotions sounds simple, it is an advanced practice. Read the following exercise first and try it only if your

WOT has expanded through pendulation and can now tolerate more discomfort. Even then, choice is extremely important for trauma healing. If you experience distress, please know that you can stop the practice at any time and use a grounding tool to return to your WOT. Despite the messages you may have heard about the importance of sitting with emotions, it's unhelpful to sit with them to the point of dysregulation; so, please be gentle with yourself.

Processing and Releasing an Emotion

As long as you are in a generally regulated state, sitting with emotions can help you learn that they're temporary experiences that can be tolerated and released.

1. You can close your eyes if it feels comfortable to do so.

2. When you're ready, check in and see if there's an emotion present.

3. Can you name it? (For example, sadness, irritability, anxiety, anger, resentment, guilt.)

4. Is there a place in your body where you feel the emotion?

5. What does it look like? Does it have a color, size, or shape?

6. Allow the feeling to be there without amplifying it. Remember to observe and be *with* it, not *in* it.

7. Breathe slowly from your diaphragm. Prolong your exhales.

8. Stay curious. Can you imagine that the emotion is a wave? Allow it to rise, peak, and fall with your slow rhythmic breaths.

9. If you like, bring to mind your own wise Higher Self. Imagine they are supporting you by helping you observe the wave.

10. Keep breathing slowly and deeply as you surf the wave of the emotion and allow it to run its course. You'll know when it's running its course because you'll feel lighter and more relaxed. (You'll find a longer list of signs of release below.)

11. Whenever you're ready, open your eyes and gently orient to the room.

You can listen to a recording of this exercise on the website for this book, http://www.newharbinger.com/53042.

Now that you've read this exercise, you may be wondering what happens when an emotion has run its course and is releasing. How do you know if you've actually moved stuck emotional energy out of your body? Keep reading.

Signs You're Actually Releasing Emotions

Any of the practices in this chapter can result in an emotional release. Here are some physiological signs that your body is discharging stress and releasing emotions.[35] Some are very subtle (such as yawning), and others are more noticeable (such as crying).

- Tears

- A big sigh

- Laughter

- Warmth

- Sweating

- Chills

- Trembling

- Yawning

- Fuller, deeper breaths

- Muscles relaxing

- A feeling of relief

- A feeling of safety or comfort

- A feeling of spaciousness or expansion

Releasing an emotion can last anywhere from a few seconds to a few minutes. As long as you're still within a tolerable range for your WOT, then it's a healthy, regulated release. Once you've released an emotion, you can stop the exercise you're working on. You can always engage in a release practice another time. Remember, this is a skill you can continue to use and build on. Some days it will be easier to release an emotion than others. Don't get discouraged if you can't always release an emotion or notice signs of a release. You're still doing a great job of building a repertoire of practices to improve your emotional health.

Releasing Stuck Stress and Tension

Because your emotions and body are intertwined, when you work on one, you work on the other. One of my favorite strategies for releasing daily stress is to simply scan my body for areas that hold tension and to use deep breathing and relaxation to release it. This practice is aptly referred to as a "wet noodle" body scan because your body feels very relaxed and loose afterward.[36] Here are some additional strategies for releasing tension and stress responses that have not been fully experienced and released.

Big Movements to Release Stress Responses

Recall the four types of stress responses from chapter 3. The fight stress response is usually associated with anger and is felt more in the arms. Flight is usually associated with anxiety and is felt more in the legs. Freeze is usually associated with shutting down or numbing out when resistance seems futile; a freeze response usually makes the body feel heavy. Fawn is responding to a threat (or perceived threat) by trying to please or be helpful.

If it feels right to you, gently explore these movements to release stress responses that might be stuck. Remember that slow is safe and give yourself space to ground or connect to areas of your body that feel stable if you need to. At some point, you might notice a sense of completion or release. Here are movements for each of the stress responses:

Fight. Push against a wall. Or make a fist with both hands; then shake them out. Next, take five deep breaths with long exhales.

Flight. Shake your body out when you're anxious. This is what animals do in the wild after running away from a predator. It will help complete the natural urge to run or escape. (Word of caution: While shaking has grown in popularity to release stuck emotions, it's important to bring awareness to shaking and to not do it mindlessly for a long time; this allows for a safe release that's within your WOT and prevents increasing activation and anxiety.) Slow the movement down and stop after a few seconds.

Freeze. Use a big bilateral stimulation practice with gentle body pats to thaw a freeze response. Hold both arms over your head. Rhythmically swing one arm down (toward your side) at a time to tap your outer thigh then bring it back up. Now switch and swing the other arm down. Keep a nice rhythmic pace while breathing slowly and intentionally. Do this slowly for a few minutes.

Fawn. Lace your fingers together behind your neck. Keep your elbows wide. Take a breath. Exhale and round your spine while bringing your elbows forward and your head down. Inhale and open your elbows wide while bringing your head up. Expand your chest wide while looking forward. Do this a few times and then keep your shoulders back as you maintain a confident posture and imagine yourself stepping into your power.

Releasing Stuck Emotional Energy Through Objects

Once you start releasing stress and emotions from your body, you'll probably discover that feeling lighter makes you more likely to notice objects that hold heavy energy in your home. Maybe it's some photos or mementos on display that no longer resonate with what you're trying to manifest. Maybe it's clothes you don't actually like or too much clutter that's holding you back from moving forward. This is a good time to start releasing old emotional energy to make room for something new.

You can use Marie Kondo's popular decluttering method to get rid of anything that doesn't "spark joy" in you.[37] This will help you release anything that holds heavy energy. Take time to make piles of things to donate, discard, and keep. Whatever method you use to declutter, make it a meaningful ritual that demonstrates your willingness to grow and surround yourself with objects that reflect your new energy.

As you release old energy and prepare for something new to come into your life, you might experience a phenomenon manifestors refer to as "tests." Next, let's do a little myth busting around the idea that the Universe is testing you and look at it in a trauma-informed way.

Manifestation Myth Busting: "The Universe Is Testing You"

There is a common belief going around that the Universe will test you to see if you'll fall back into old patterns when you are trying to manifest something new. Unfortunately, the idea that the Universe might be evaluating (or worse, tricking) you can be triggering for trauma survivors. But there is another way to look at so-called tests. Sometimes when we are actively trying to manifest a goal, we'll get presented with opportunities that seem good, but are not quite healthy for us. Maybe it's an ex or an old job that seems to have improved. Maybe it's a new romantic interest or job opportunity that sounds good but is actually remarkably similar to our past patterns. We want it to work, but deep down we know that it's not right for us. To manifest *successfully*, you don't have to believe that the Universe is testing you to see if you'll take the bait or are ready to level up; instead, you can see it as an old pattern that is stopping by to say good-bye as it gets energetically cleared away and released. Say good-bye and keep moving!

Now that you've started the process of releasing stuck emotions that can block manifesting, you're going to explore the root cause of many stuck emotions: attachment injuries. Your relational wounds from childhood can create patterns of behavior that interfere with manifesting because you're still preoccupied with surviving rather than thriving. The next chapter will help you break free and find security within.

Take-Home Points

- Trauma can cause emotions to get stuck in our bodies.

- Our window of tolerance is the key to regulating emotions.

- When we release emotions in a regulated way, we feel lighter.

- When we feel safer and lighter, we make room to manifest something new.

CHAPTER 5

Reparent Yourself for a Secure Attachment Style

The way we move forward is to have the awareness that we can become the wise parent to ourselves that we did not have as a child.

—Dr. Nicole LePera, *How to Do the Work*

Carolyn had a pattern of sacrificing herself in order to make everyone around her comfortable. At work, she felt responsible for her manager's mood and went out of her way to please him. At home, her mind was preoccupied with the stability of her marriage—she often felt anxious and avoided conflict at all costs. She struggled with boundaries with her children, not realizing that her overhelping and constant worrying only pushed them away. As a child, Carolyn didn't have stable relationships with her own parents. They were focused on problems in their marriage and provided inconsistent warmth and attention. One day, her father suddenly left home and moved across the country with a female coworker. It wasn't until Carolyn's own kids went to college that she realized how her fear of abandonment impacted her relationships and goals. She began giving her husband and kids more independence and started taking care of her own needs, including her health. She even reached a goal that had always eluded her: to become fit and take hiking tours in Europe, including the Camino de Santiago trail across northern Spain.

Trauma, especially relational trauma in childhood, can cause you to overfocus on other people in order to manage threats and maintain safety. Healing is an invitation to attend to yourself while learning to feel safe from the inside out. Of course relationships matter, and we'll get to ones that support healing, but your relationship with yourself is primary because it has the power to heal your past and manifest your future. Even as an adult, it's never too late to recognize your unmet needs from childhood and to start providing them for yourself. Doing so can change your life trajectory—allowing you to release old patterns that no longer serve you and reach levels of manifestation you didn't think were possible. Rather than overattending to things you can't control—other people—and feeling helpless, you can reconnect with your own sense of agency and power.

It's important to have compassion for the younger parts of you that focus on others in order to maintain safety. It makes sense if you've become hypervigilant to connection and disconnection if your survival in childhood depended on unpredictable, neglectful, or unsafe caregivers. You probably had to be attentive to others—alert to their moods and behaviors—so you could assess what's happening and whether you were safe or your needs would be met. As an adult, you can create new patterns. What does that look like from a practical perspective? It means that if, for example, you get triggered by an ex or someone who hurt you on social media, you don't follow the old path of fixating on them and doubting your self-worth. It means you turn all that attention back to supporting yourself and becoming the primary caretaker of the wounded parts of yourself. You can do what developer of Internal Family Systems trauma therapy Dr. Richard Schwartz calls a *radical U-turn*, or *you-turn*.[38] In the you-turn, you bring curiosity and compassion to your reactions rather than focus on the behaviors of other people.

I believe that with enough repetitions, your new you-turns will help avoid activating the neural pathways responsible for self-abandonment. This type of commitment takes some work, and I don't suggest it lightly. I realize how hard it is to use willpower to change a trauma response and I won't ask you to do it anywhere else in this book. It takes intentional effort to override patterns that have been embedded for such a long time.

This one is important, however. It will make the difference between living at the level of survival as you grasp at external sources of security, and living at the level of self-trust and self-worth when you find security within.

If you're like Carolyn, you might overfocus on others to your own detriment. Depending on your attachment style, this might look like being other-focused in your day-to-day life or in your imagination. It might also mean that you try to keep people close, push them away, or both. The following list can help you identify if overfocusing on others is a problem for you. Do you:

- Monitor ex-partners on social media?

- Spend too much time or energy helping others?

- Have a fantasy bond with a "perfect" partner you haven't met yet?

- Obsess about your children's education?

- Experience an excessive amount of jealousy?

- Fantasize about relationships while avoiding intimacy in real life?

- Constantly seek validation or admiration from others?

- Become preoccupied with your partner?

- Engage in snowplow or helicopter parenting?

- Compete with people on social media?

- Try to regulate everyone's emotions?

- Fixate on someone you idealize, hero-worship, or envy?

- Believe that other people's needs are more important than your own?

- Have trouble setting and enforcing boundaries?

- Try to win arguments with people in your head?

- Excessively criticize or blame others?

- Fantasize about someone rescuing you?

- Try to prove your worth to people who hurt you?

- Try to heal people who hurt you?

- Try to get people who hurt you to heal you?

If you've experienced many of the items on the list, it's likely that you spend a lot of time and energy trying to manage closeness in order to feel safe. When you feel the urge to overfocus on others, you may not recognize the experience for what it is: Each one is a fight, flight, freeze, or fawn trauma response, and all are attempts to cope with dysregulation that stems from childhood attachment wounds. Focusing on others in an excessive way usually indicates an insecure attachment style.

What Is an Attachment Style?

Your attachment style is the way you approach connection and closeness. It's based on your experiences with caregivers, and it can be a reflection of how you learned to cope with their limitations. Since you were dependent on your caregivers as a child, you might have adapted to even intolerable situations in order to survive. There are four attachment styles; one is considered secure, and the other three are insecure. Let's get to know each style and how it develops.

Secure Attachment

According to Dr. Daniel Siegel, secure attachment is fostered by feeling seen, safe, soothed, and secure. He calls these the "four Ss."[39] If you have a secure attachment style, you probably felt seen because your caregivers paid attention to you and validated your feelings. They were emotionally available and kept you safe. Although they weren't perfect, you knew they were capable of repairing the relationship when conflicts arose. No matter how big your feelings were, you felt soothed by their ability to provide healthy co-regulation. As a result of feeling seen, safe, and soothed, you probably feel comfortable with connection and with being alone. You probably don't see relationships as hard work, and you're reliable and flexible. You communicate in a healthy way and aren't afraid of commitment. You're able to see from different perspectives and imagine different possibilities. Ultimately, your sense of security allows you to give and receive love comfortably.

When it comes to the nervous system and manifesting, this attachment style is ventral vagal dominant. You feel regulated most of the time, and your approach to manifesting is mostly confident and resilient. Since it's possible to change your attachment style when you heal—called *earned secure attachment*—this style is most consistent with the self-healer manifestor type.

Anxious Attachment

If you have an anxious attachment style, you probably had caregivers who were inconsistent or unpredictable. Sometimes they were attentive and caring, and other times they were distracted, unreliable, or intrusive. As a result, you weren't sure if you were loved or if your needs were going to be met. If you have this style, you're probably hypervigilant about any signs of rejection or loss of connection. You're preoccupied with relationships and believe you have to work hard to keep them. You worry that small acts will ruin them, and you live in fear of abandonment. You need reassurance and struggle with being alone.

When it comes to the nervous system and manifesting, anxious attachment leans toward dysregulation and is considered sympathetic dominant. It is most consistent with the hustler manifestor type, which looks like trying to control outcomes, extreme effort, and an anxious preoccupation with what you're trying to manifest.

Avoidant Attachment

If you have an avoidant attachment style, you probably had caregivers who were neglectful and perhaps rejecting. They didn't provide you with emotional support or safety. Despite lacking emotional presence, they might have been more available when teaching you a task. As a result of not having your needs met, you developed mistrust and extreme self-reliance. If you have this style, you probably value independence and boundaries. This doesn't mean, however, that you don't want relationships and connection. It means you struggle with vulnerability and distance yourself from others to feel safe. Because connection feels overwhelming, you engage in behaviors that promote disconnection. This might include devaluing others, distracting yourself with activities, and fantasizing about a "perfect" romance.

When it comes to the nervous system and manifesting, avoidant attachment leans toward dysregulation and is considered dorsal vagal dominant. It is most consistent with the daydreamer manifestor type, which looks like feeling stuck, fantasizing about perfect outcomes, struggling with taking action, and not asking for help with goals.

Disorganized Attachment

If you have a disorganized attachment style, your caregiver was probably a source of extreme distress or fear. They may have been abusive or struggled with mental health in a way that made them frightened or frightening. The problem this presented to your developing nervous system and brain is that it activated two opposing circuits: one that makes you want to get away from threat, and one that makes you seek out your attachment figure to be soothed and protected. This is confusing because you can't get away from and run toward the same person. If you have this style, you might experience extreme swings between anxious attachment behaviors and avoidant attachment behaviors. You often feel triggered and unsafe with others. You tend to develop love-hate relationships and struggle with having a stable sense of self.

When it comes to the nervous system and manifesting, disorganized attachment represents chronic dysregulation in the form of extreme and sudden shifts in nervous system arousal. Rather than being sympathetic or dorsal dominant, there's an oscillation between the two. This is experienced as extreme increases and decreases in energy, often in response to relational triggers. Disorganized attachment is most consistent with the complex manifestor type, which looks like sudden shifts between anxiously chasing goals and feeling helpless and hopeless about achieving them.

You Make Sense

If your attachment style is insecure, you're not alone. In the United States, about 50 percent of people experience insecure attachment.[40] Fortunately, you can heal your attachment trauma and develop what's called an *earned secure attachment*. One of the most effective ways to do this is to make sense of your past and how it's affected you. As Dr. Daniel Siegel points out, "When we create a narrative of who we are, we link past and present so we can become the active author of a possible future, too."[41]

You might have had an insecure upbringing, but you can still have a secure story—meaning you understand what happened to you and how it affects your attachment style today. You can see how this might be relevant to manifesting. If you can look back on your past with some compassion and clarity, it can help you recognize which needs were unmet. By providing these needs today, you can create the future you want.

To illustrate, let's look at how Aditi created a brighter future by reflecting on her life story. For a long time, Aditi didn't think about her inner life because it was hard to recall parts of her childhood. On her healing journey, she learned safe ways to connect to internal sensations, emotions and, eventually, some memories. She realized that she had a disorganized attachment style, and it explained why she struggled with emotion dysregulation, developed intense but short relationships, dissociated often, and had gaps in her memory. Her parents were cruel and, on occasion, physically abusive. While she let herself believe that they weren't perfect, she now identified them as abusive. This new story liberated her from years of self-blame, which was a survival strategy she developed in order to preserve a connection with the attachment figures she had no choice but to depend on as a child. While the new story required some processing and grieving, it allowed a younger version of herself to finally feel seen. Aditi felt more committed than ever to helping the younger versions of herself feel safe and soothed through protective boundaries and emotion regulation. This commitment allowed her to create healthier relationships and more emotional balance.

Understanding your attachment style can be beneficial, but it can be difficult to look at your whole attachment story all at once when you have a heavy trauma burden. The following journaling exercise is designed to help you make sense of your attachment style. Use it if you feel resourced enough and take a break if you feel too dysregulated by the questions. If this exercise is too triggering, it may be best to skip it.

Your Attachment Needs

This journaling exercise invites you to explore whether your attachment needs were met in childhood and what your current attachment style looks like. Use a journal to answer the following questions:

1. As a child, did you feel seen, safe, or soothed by your caregivers?

2. Do you know why your caregivers acted the way they did? Are there any lineage wounds you know about?

3. What attachment style do you resonate with the most?

4. How did your childhood influence this style?

Looking back at your family experiences in childhood can help you understand the parents you had and the parents you needed. There are probably younger parts of you that still need to feel seen, safe, soothed, and secure. Let's give those parts of yourself some attention.

Being the Parent You Needed

The process of attuning to your unmet needs and providing them for yourself is called *reparenting*. In chapter 1, you were introduced to the idea that you can be a nonjudgmental witness to your experience. You worked on your ability to observe your thoughts and emotions in a mindful way. By awakening this witness perspective, you are on your way to tapping into a still, eternal aspect of yourself that can be your source of reparenting. This inner self is a well of wisdom, and it has been called many names including your core self, your authentic self, your adult self, your higher self, your divine self, your inner being, your soul and, in the Internal Family Systems (IFS) model of therapy, your Self. In IFS, the Self is an innate divine essence inside of us. It doesn't need to be cultivated, and it can't be harmed. Not only is it untouched by trauma, it can be a source of healing it. IFS developer Dr. Dick Schwartz explains that while the Self can notice your internal experiences, it is not content to passively observe.[42] When you access your Self, you realize that it wants to help you. It wants to heal you.

By anchoring your awareness to Self, you can embody the qualities it expresses. These qualities are referred to as the eight Cs.

- Curiosity

- Confidence

- Calm

- Compassion

- Creativity

- Courage

- Clarity

- Connectedness

When you experience these qualities, you have what's called "Self-energy." It's when you're in a ventral vagal state and feel safe. To reparent wounded, younger parts of yourself—what is sometimes called your inner child—you need to have enough Self-energy. The goal of IFS is to access this energy more often and become Self-led. Being Self-led means that your Self has become the wise inner parent to all the different parts of your personality. We'll talk more about these different personality parts—including how they are burdened by trauma and how they affect manifesting our goals—in the next two chapters. For now, it's important to understand that the Self is a natural source of reparenting and healing. That's why IFS is sometimes described as internal attachment work. Secure attachment can be an inside job when your parts trust in your Self to take care of them.

How can you access Self-energy and show your wounded inner child that you are capable of being there for them now? One starting point is to build on your nervous system regulation practices. When you notice that you feel dysregulated, gently attend to any needs that might be coming up.

For example, let's say you just received a rejection email from a school or job you had your heart set on. You feel deeply hurt and notice that you're getting out of your WOT. You have an urge to overfocus on others—to devalue the company or school and whomever they chose to accept or hire. But then you remember that you can take a few deep breaths and choose to reparent yourself instead. To meet your need to be seen, you accept and validate your feelings of disappointment. Next, you decide to self-soothe by doing something nice for yourself. You read a few chapters in a fun fantasy novel and then go for a walk. To feel safe, you remind yourself that you're resourceful and will continue to send out applications. The rejection still hurts, but you feel more secure knowing that you can take good care of yourself.

Here is an exercise to help you meet your needs and feel more secure.

Security from the Inside Out

When you feel triggered and have an urge to overfocus on someone else, try to interrupt the pattern and do a "you-turn." Just notice if there's a need related to security coming up. Gently and compassionately put the focus back on supporting yourself and the younger parts of you that need security right now. Ask yourself the following questions and see if there's a healthy action you can take to address an unmet need:

- How can I help myself feel chosen right now? (For example, turning your attention toward your inner child rather than the person who triggered you.)

- How can I help myself feel seen and heard right now? (For example, telling an anxious part of yourself that it makes sense and you understand it.)

- How can I help myself feel safe and protected right now? (For example, setting and enforcing a needed boundary with someone.)

- How can I help myself feel soothed right now? (For example, taking a few deep breaths and stretching and relaxing to release tension from your body.)

- How can I help myself feel reparented? (For example, reminding your inner child that you are there for them so they don't feel exiled and alone.)

Once you get in the habit of accessing Self in small moments of nervous system regulation and using it as a resource for reparenting your inner child, you might wonder if there is something beyond this divine essence that you can rely on—maybe something bigger, such as your relationship to the Universe.

Your Attachment Style to the Universe

Traditional psychology tends to focus on our attachment style to our primary caregivers, but there is a whole body of psychological research that studies our attachment style to the Divine. In research, it's often referred to as *divine attachment* or *attachment to God*. In this book, I'll use these terms and *attachment to the Universe* interchangeably.

If you have a secure attachment style, you can say, "Yes!" to Einstein's famous question, "Is the Universe friendly?" You feel safe and trust in a benevolent Universe. Studies show that people with a secure attachment style are more likely to report a secure attachment to God.[43] They see God as available and responsive and turn to God in times of distress. They also draw confidence from God to explore the world.

And if you have an insecure attachment style, there are two well-researched yet conflicting models regarding how you attach to the Universe. The first model, called the *correspondence hypothesis*, states that your attachment style informs your attachment to the Universe. If you have an anxious attachment style, for example, you'll also have an anxious attachment to the Universe. The second model is called the *compensation hypothesis*. According to this model, your attachment to the Universe compensates for insecure human attachment. You can have a secure attachment to the Universe even if you didn't have it with your caregivers. There are four reasons you might turn to the Universe as a substitute attachment figure:[44]

1. You experienced severe stress or trauma and perceived your attachment figures as inadequate to help you.

2. Your primary attachment figure became unavailable, especially as a result of loss, death, divorce, or separation.

3. You have an insecure attachment history from childhood and therefore seek the Universe as a surrogate attachment figure.

4. You have an insecure romantic attachment style as an adult and turn to the Universe because you are dissatisfied with romantic relationships.

If the Universe is a surrogate attachment figure for you, you're not alone. The Universe is the ultimate source of security for many people, but that doesn't make it any less real. The more important question for your healing is whether your relationship to the Universe is helpful. Which attachment style to the Universe do you resonate with the most?

•   If you trust that the Universe is available and responsive, you probably have a secure attachment to it.

•   If you have an anxious attachment style to the Universe, you're more likely to see it as inconsistently available and responsive. You seek out connection but worry about whether the Universe is there for you.

•   If you have an avoidant attachment style to the Universe, you're likely to see it as distant and inaccessible. You don't feel emotionally supported by it and tend to cope on your own.

- As for a disorganized attachment style to the Universe, you sometimes see it as inconsistently available and responsive and, at other times, distant and inaccessible. You have a very hard time trusting that the Universe is a safe haven for you.

Keep in mind that your attachment style to humans and to the Universe are not diagnoses. They are flexible models of how you try to get your needs met and can change. For example, countless studies show that those with an insecure attachment style to caregivers in childhood are more likely to undergo sudden and dramatic spiritual changes in adulthood and to convert to new religions or to New Age spirituality.[45] Those who identify as New Age are especially more likely to have had an insecure attachment style to caregivers in childhood.[46] In other words, if you didn't get your attachment needs met in childhood, you can actively look for a more supportive relationship with the Universe in adulthood.

Even if you do form a healthy relationship with the Universe, there are times in your healing or manifestation journey that you might struggle with it. In research, these are called *religious/spiritual struggles*. Some of the women in my doctoral dissertation research on infertility and spirituality experienced this type of conflict. They felt angry and betrayed or punished by the Divine because of infertility. Maybe you've felt betrayed or punished by the Universe too. Maybe you've been waiting so long for something to manifest that your connection with the Universe is not a supportive relationship for you. Perhaps you've lost trust. Perhaps you never had trust in the Universe.

How do you begin to rebuild or recreate your relationship to the Universe? How do you experience the deep trust that could be possible with secure attachment? After two decades of working with people who experience spiritual struggles and experiencing them myself, I've discovered that the keys to healing the relationship are connection and repair.

Connection

To have a secure relationship with the Universe, you need the *felt sense of connection* to it. It's not simply a thought, but a feeling in your being and in your body. One of the best ways to experience this feeling is in nature. This is true even if we aren't the outdoorsy type. As a teen living in the inner city, I loved to look up at the sky when things got tough and gaze at the mystery—clouds floating by or stars twinkling off in the distance, faintly breaking through city lights. Anything that reminded me of something bigger than myself.

In *Awe: The New Science of Everyday Wonder and How It Can Transform Your Life*, author and professor of psychology at UC Berkeley Dr. Dacher Keltner defines awe as "the feeling of being in the presence of something vast that transcends your current understanding of the world."[47] Often a spiritual or religious emotion, awe is how you feel when you're amazed at things outside yourself. It's a felt sense because it is often accompanied by bodily responses such as tears, chills, *whoas*, and *wows*. While fleeting, moments of transcendence can have a significant impact on your mental and physical health and your connection to the Divine. According to Keltner, Americans often sense the Divine in nature. When you encounter vast mysteries in nature, you can experience awe, and it can connect you to the Divine. You can feel guided by the flows of a river or allow your sense of a small self to dissolve into a field of grass on a sunny day. Anything that lets you feel closer to and, if possible, held by the Universe.

Repair

If your relationship to the Universe is truly a relationship, then the experience of repair is necessary for security. When you are struggling with spirituality, especially as a result of struggling with manifesting something important to you, I offer you this: If you can't find the Universe, ask it to find you. No matter how angry, resentful, or distant you've felt from the Universe, it can take it. It's safe to tell the Divine that it let you down and to ask for a repair. This can involve an inner dialogue, a prayer, or a down-on-your-knees cry if that's what feels right. You can say, "Universe, I need you to make amends with me and show me your ability to repair our bond." Then let it go. Stay open and don't expect any particular response. I use this practice sparingly with incredible, sometimes miraculous results in a short period of time. The Universe will respond, maybe in a life-changing conversation with a stranger or a sudden solution to an insurmountable problem. Maybe with a tear-filled experience of awe that renders you speechless. When you're ready, simply ask the Universe to find you.

Healthy Relationships

Author Dr. Gabor Maté states, "Safety is not the absence of threat, but the presence of connection."[48] To have a felt sense of safety, it's important to start connecting with yourself, the Universe if possible, and supportive others. Over time, these connections can transform your attachment style.

Healthy relationships to supportive people are an important part of the equation but can be tricky to navigate. The difficulty with healthy relationships is that they might not appeal to you if you're struggling with attachment trauma. Attachment trauma can push you to gravitate toward unhealthy relationships because they feel familiar, and it's natural to mistake familiarity with safety. You might also be attracted to unhealthy relationships because there's a younger part of you that wants to have a corrective experience.

Unfortunately, unhealthy relationships rarely offer the healing you're seeking. Instead, you might end up in a *trauma bond*, where you become deeply attached and loyal to a hurtful relationship because of attachment wounds. Lost in a trance of hope, you might cling to the other person's potential to love you properly while you wait for a miracle. Others can see their hurtful behavior for what it is, but you might just see their wounded inner child and use it to excuse their behavior. Meanwhile, they don't see yours and can't meet your emotional needs.

If you're struggling to choose healthy relationships, it's time to do a you-turn and advocate for your wounded inner child. What type of people does it need to be around to thrive? To feel seen, heard, and safe? If you aren't getting any of these needs met, it's important to take a look at your relationships. Do you need to learn how to ask for what you want? To set boundaries? To make time for friends? To add a therapist or healthy people to your life? Or to consider leaving toxic relationships? (Please seek professional help if you're in an abusive relationship because leaving one is a particularly dangerous time.)

At the end of the day, your relationships reflect adaptive strategies that may or may not be working anymore. Learning to identify your needs will help you see whether changes are necessary. In the next chapter, we'll look at the things your wounded inner child still needs and explore the ways it uses manifesting to try to meet those needs. And, of course, we'll discuss how reparenting can help you course correct when your wounded inner child's desires lead to unhealthy patterns.

Take-Home Points

- Your attachment style is not a diagnosis, and it can change.

- Attending to your needs to be seen, safe, and soothed is a part of reparenting yourself.

- You can work on your attachment to the Universe by connecting to it in nature and asking it to connect to you through repair.

- Supportive relationships are an important part of developing a secure attachment style.

CHAPTER 6

Explore What Your Inner Child Wants You to Manifest

Toxic ties undermine and weaken our vision of what is possible in our lives.

—Katherine Woodward Thomas, *Calling in "The One"*

Marissa longed to get back together with her ex. Instead of focusing on how verbally abusive and emotionally unavailable he was, she reminisced about how she felt when he "love-bombed" her. She missed the flattery and attention and convinced herself that if he came back and stayed, it would prove that she's lovable. One day, she saw a video offering a method to attract your ex. It was a manifestation practice called the "whisper method." The whisper method involves visualizing yourself walking up to your "sp," or specific person, usually an ex or a crush, and whispering a command in their ear. After whispering the command, something along the lines of, "You find me irresistible," you kiss them on the cheek and walk away without looking back. Even though a small still voice inside told Marissa that getting back together with her ex was a bad idea, she tried the method immediately. To her surprise, he texted two days later desperate to reunite.

It took less than a week for Marissa to realize that her boyfriend hadn't changed at all. She repeated the pattern of breaking up and getting back together for months before she was ready to end the cycle. Once she did, she decided to stop using the whisper method. Instead, she wanted to manifest a healthy relationship by focusing on healing herself so she no longer yearned for toxic relationships. A year later, she began to date men who valued her and treated her with respect.

Almost everyone knows what longing for something we know isn't good for us feels like: it's intoxicating. You're not sure why you want it, but the sense of urgency to possess it courses through your body like nothing else. Maybe you want to date the attractive guy you met online even though he's shown you he lacks empathy. Maybe you want the high-powered job even though you hate the day-to-day work involved. Maybe you want the extravagant trips to impress your friends even if it means you'll go into debt. These are the type of goals we looked at in chapter 2: wound-based goals. You might rationally know that value-based goals would make you happier, but something inside probably still feels vulnerable to the tug of wound-based goals.

It's important to explore where these wound-based goals come from so you don't spend years trying to attain things that ultimately limit you. Once you start exploring, you'll likely get to the source of your stuck patterns and longings: your wounded inner child.

Manifesting isn't always fun visualization practices, moon rituals, and requests to the Universe. Sometimes it's tapping into your unconscious mind so you can let go of what's keeping you from thriving. Your wounded inner child is the most unconscious part of you. It's deeply buried because accessing it can be overwhelming. That's why we're going to slowly build a relationship to it. First, let's look at what your inner child actually is.

What Exactly Is Your Inner Child?

When I say inner child, I'm actually referring to multiple inner child parts, or inner children. These are the younger versions of yourself. Maybe it's your five-year-old self, your ten-year-old self, or your sixteen-year-old self. It's easiest to recognize these parts when you're triggered. For example, you might notice that when something stressful happens, you suddenly feel like a frightened toddler or an angry teenager. In these moments, you emotionally regress back to an early age or stage. This is why it can be helpful to ask yourself, "How old do I feel right now?" when you're triggered. Once you get to know your parts, you might want to ask, "What part of me is activated right now?"

There are many psychology models that acknowledge the idea that we have different "parts" to our personality, or subpersonalities. Working with these subpersonalities is called "parts work." The Internal Family Systems (IFS) model explains parts in clear ways and offers a powerful path to healing. You might recall the Self in IFS from chapter 5. It's the core of who you are, and it can reparent all of your parts, including your inner child. In addition to the Self, there are two categories of parts in the IFS model: protector parts and exiled parts. As you'll see, your parts really are like members of a family that have their own roles.

Protector Parts

There are two types of protectors: managers and firefighters.

Managers. Managers are your first line of defense. They are proactive in trying to stop your wounded inner child from being activated. They are often task-oriented and help you function in your daily life. Examples include your inner critic, a people pleaser part, a perfectionistic part, and a worrying part. These parts are relevant to manifesting because they can be driven to succeed, worry about outcomes, keep you from taking action, and try to control the process of manifesting.

Firefighters. Firefighters are your emergency response workers. They are your second line of defense. They are reactive and will do anything to distract you from a wounded inner child part that has been triggered. Their job is to extinguish the flames when the emotional pain of your inner child comes to the surface. Examples include a part that binge-eats, a part that numbs out by scrolling on social media, a part that dissociates when traumatic memories come up, a part that abuses substances, and a sexually addicted part. If you try to rush healing or don't get the consent of your protectors to access traumatic memories, firefighters will come to the rescue and take over. This is called *backlash*, and it may lead to an increase in harmful behaviors.

This is why it's important to not try to bypass protectors and work with traumatic memories without a trained trauma therapist. Firefighter parts are relevant to manifesting because their actions can negatively impact your goals. While they're not trying to sabotage you, their protective efforts come from a sense of urgency and can have unintended harmful consequences.

It's important to remember that your protectors use adaptive survival strategies. They're working hard to try to help you by using approaches that worked in the past. In fact, all of your protectors have positive intentions. The goal is not to get rid of them, but to understand them and show them compassion. Despite outward appearances, they use their roles to keep you safe. The problem is that they can disagree with each other and cause harm when their protective efforts have consequences. In the next chapter, you'll learn tools for resolving inner conflicts when these parts pull you in opposite directions and further away from achieving your goals.

Here is a quick exercise to get to know one of your protectors, a manager part we all know well: the inner critic. The inner critic's role is to criticize and shame you and your other parts. Despite its outward appearance, it has a positive intention. It's trying to keep you in line and get you to improve yourself. It believes that doing so will protect you from being judged or rejected by others.

Get to Know Your Inner Critic

I invite you to explore your inner critic and its role by answering the following questions. You can close your eyes if you'd like. Simply ask the question and try not to think of an answer. Just see what pops up. Use a journal to keep track of your answers. To start, get a sense of your inner critic. Perhaps you can recall a recent time when it's been activated and you noticed critical self-talk.

- Where do you feel your inner critic in your body?

- What does it look like?

- Ask it how it is trying to help you.

- How does it do this job?

- What is it worried will happen if it doesn't do this job?

- If it could have any other job, what would it like to do?

What was this exercise like for you? Was it easy or challenging to listen for answers? Were you surprised by the answers your inner critic provided? Is this conversation something you'd like to do with other protector parts? (In the next chapter, you'll have a longer list of protector parts you might want to connect to and dialogue with.) Whatever information you received, remember that any time you try to have a better relationship with your inner parts, you're taking a big step toward your healing and transformation. Give yourself a big dose of self-compassion no matter what you find.

Exiled Parts

Exiles are your vulnerable, injured, scared parts that hold your most painful emotions and memories, and are banished out of your awareness for your protection. They are often younger and what I refer to when I say "wounded inner child." They may have been neglected, shamed, abused, othered, dismissed, or abandoned. The more trauma you have, the more exiles you have. The more exiles you have, the harder your protectors have to work. Exiles are stuck in time and hold wound-based feelings (such as sadness after being rejected) and beliefs (such as I am worthless). They have many unmet needs and subsequent longings that can result in the toxic patterns and wound-based goals that hold you back. They can also carry the core wounds that are the root cause of your struggles with manifestation. We often discover this when we ask ourselves, "When did I first learn that getting money (or love, or whatever you're trying to manifest) is hard?"

If thinking about your own exiles and longings feels heavy, I get it. We exile them away precisely because thinking about them can feel like too much. This might be a good time to take a few intentional deep breaths and ground yourself in the present moment. Drop your shoulders and use long exhales to release any feelings that might be coming up. Remember, the purpose of learning about your unmet needs isn't to revisit the past (working with traumatic memories is ideally done in the presence of a trauma therapist). It's to validate and acknowledge the challenges and struggles you've had and how they might be affecting you today. Our patterns are often our unconscious blind spots. The more aware we become, the easier it is to change them and to manifest the life we want. If it feels too heavy to do the exercises, it's absolutely okay to learn about inner child healing on an intellectual level until you're ready to try it. You'll still get the benefit of greater insight.

You are not alone if your inner child has wounds that are affecting you today. Unmet needs and their subsequent longings create patterns that impact how you approach manifesting. Sometimes they show up as your inner child still trying to get the need met. Other times it looks like your protectors doing whatever they can to manage or hide the wound. Let's explore a few common ways your inner child wounds might show up in manifesting. Along with the wounds, I'll offer some related affirmations you can use to nurture your inner child.

Yearn to be chosen. We all want someone to "choose" us—to make us feel loved, valued, and wanted. Sometimes, this need goes unmet, and we fall into a pattern of trying to be chosen. If your caregivers' emotional or physical presence was unavailable, inconsistent, or suddenly lost during childhood, you might have experienced an abandonment wound that made you feel like you weren't chosen. This is especially common when caregiver attention is suddenly limited or you experience the loss of a caregiver through separation, divorce, incarceration, or death. If you have this wound, your inner child may try to manifest or chase relationships with unavailable people or institutions. They might be unavailable to you because they're already taken, emotionally unavailable, not interested, or a bad fit or match for you.

Affirmation: *I choose you, little one.* (Try using a pet name, such as little one or sweetheart for your inner child, if it helps.)

Yearn to be seen. We all want to be acknowledged, understood, and accepted. And yet, our caregivers might not see the real us at all. Maybe they were too busy or self-involved to have noticed or celebrated our successes. Or they might have dismissed our opinions or disapproved of our choices or the things that made us happy. Perhaps they bought into toxic cultural messages around achievement and made us feel like our value was based on what we did, not who we are. If your caregivers didn't meet your emotional need to be seen and heard, your inner child might chase or seek to manifest the experience of being seen through high performance, achievement, prestige, beauty, success, money, power, or celebrity status.

Affirmation: *I see you. I hear you.*

Yearn to be saved. We all have a need to be taken care of by the people we depend on as children. When the need doesn't get met, we can continue to seek it out. If you felt vulnerable, neglected, helpless, powerless, or traumatized in childhood, your inner child might seek the experience of being rescued and taken care of emotionally or financially. This can show up as fantasizing about, and trying to manifest, an idealized relationship (such as someone who automatically understands and takes care of all your needs) or a magical solution to problems (winning the lottery, for example) rather than taking action to make changes.

Affirmation: *I'm here to take care of you now.*

Yearn to be soothed. As children, we all have a need to be comforted. If your caregivers didn't soothe you when you were scared or distressed, your inner child might continue to seek temporary relief from emotional discomfort through coping strategies that are compulsive or hard to control. This can show up as behaviors that interfere with manifesting goals. For example, you might soothe yourself through emotional eating even though it conflicts with your goal to improve your health. Or you might soothe yourself with shopping splurges even though your goal is to save for a big trip.

Affirmation: *It's okay. I'm here for you.*

Yearn to feel safe. We all have a basic need to be safe from harm. If you didn't experience safety or protection in childhood, your inner child might seek to feel powerful in a variety of ways. Perhaps it's through positions of power, money, physical fitness, aloofness, sarcasm, bullying, or befriending bullies. If you have this wound, your inner child might even seek out narcissists and dangerous people despite your rational desire for healthy relationships. This often happens if you had to fawn to someone threatening in childhood in order to stay safe. Either it helped you escape their aggressive behavior or being associated with them protected you from others. This can show up in adulthood as a pattern of being drawn to and appeasing narcissistic partners and friends. While the partner or friend can make you feel safe because of their ruthless or intimidating behavior toward others, safety in the relationship requires walking on eggshells and self-abandonment as you try to appease them.

Affirmation: *I'm here to protect you, to keep you safe.*

Marissa, from the earlier example, yearned to be chosen and to feel safe. As a child, she felt invisible except when she performed exceptionally well in school. While her parents were wealthy and provided a comfortable lifestyle, they were emotionally absent. Her friends often joked that they were "about as warm as an ATM machine." What they didn't know was that her parents had a lot of narcissistic traits and could be scary when Marissa didn't agree with them or meet their expectations. Once she recognized her inner child's needs to feel chosen and safe, Marissa started providing these needs to herself. She began to feel tenderness for her wounded inner child and wanted to protect it from toxic relationships. She took her time dating to find someone who was a healthy match and eventually married a man who was warm and accepting.

As you can see, Marissa stopped acting on her inner child's longings and started having a relationship with it. In IFS, when a part of us (an inner child part in Marissa's case), takes the driver's seat in our psyche and we identify with it and act from it, it's called *blending*. Blending with our parts can be habitual, and if we're blended with fearful inner child parts, the world can feel like a scary place. Blending with wounded inner child parts can make it feel as though past trauma is happening in the present. Learning how to unblend can give you *dual awareness* of both the past and present, your activated parts' feelings, and your current adult feelings at the same time. Unblending with parts is one of the most useful tools you could ever acquire, and I'm excited to introduce you to it. Let's look at unblending more closely.

Unblend from Your Inner Child

To understand unblending, notice the difference between "I'm scared that my dream won't work out" and "A part of me is scared that this dream won't work out." When you are blended, you are consumed by a part and its feelings. If you can separate from it and acknowledge the feeling as a part's feeling, you are better able to witness and soothe its fear rather than act on it. If it's an inner child part, you can also recognize how small it is compared to your adult self and feel compassion and protectiveness toward it. Additionally, you might see that there are other parts of you that aren't scared.

You might notice that unblending feels very similar to the techniques you learned earlier that helped you mindfully observe your feelings rather than get consumed by them. Unblending helps you separate not only from a feeling but also from the part of you that holds the feeling.

For example, Sam worked in tech and was trying to manifest more financial abundance. She felt surprised and triggered when she lost her job due to a temporary wave of layoffs. She grew up in poverty, and losing her job activated a wounded inner child that held feelings of powerlessness and helplessness. After hearing about the layoff, she sat on the couch and zoned out. Several hours later, her dog came over and comforted her, which helped her feel grounded. In that moment, she remembered something she heard about inner child healing on a podcast. She decided to give it a try. She asked her inner child to step back so she could show it compassion. It did, and she realized it was her five-year-old "little Sam" part that didn't know how to help her parents with their money problems. She told the young part that it makes sense that she couldn't help them because she was just a child. She told little Sam that she was an adult now and capable of looking for another job. Little Sam felt comforted, and

Sam suddenly felt unstuck and mobilized. She got up from the couch and started applying for jobs.

Ultimately, the distinction between a blended state and an unblended state is that in a blended state, you're consumed by a distressed or activated part and its feelings. In an unblended state, you can have a relationship to the part.

It's natural to get swept up and blended with your parts' strong feelings. Give yourself compassion when you first become aware of this tendency. Learning how to unblend is a skill you have to practice to master. Use these tips to help you mindfully notice a part as a part rather than automatically identify with its feelings.

- Get in the habit of saying, "A part of me feels…" and "A part of me thinks…"

- Recognize signs that you're blended with a protective part: judgment, criticism, perfectionism, addictive behaviors, avoidance, some physical symptoms, and aggression toward yourself or others.

- Recognize signs that you're blended with an exiled or wounded inner child part: extreme fear, helplessness, shame, hopelessness, sadness, or worthlessness. You might also feel very sensitive and exposed.

- You can use the nervous system regulation skills from chapter 3 to get more regulated before trying to have a dialogue with any part. This will help you be in a ventral vagal state and have more Self-energy so you can be curious and compassionate.

- Instead of using regulation skills, you can just ask the part to step back and not overwhelm you so you're able to give it compassion. Parts are often relieved to hear that they don't have to take over in order to get your attention.

- Mindfully separate from the part or ask it to separate from you so you can give it compassion and hear what it needs. If it's an inner child part, perhaps it needs to feel safe, soothed, seen, or heard in this moment. Once it steps back, make sure to follow through and provide the safety, comfort, or validation it needs. Don't underestimate the power of validating a part's feelings.

- If you're having trouble unblending, try to locate a part of you that's the opposite of the part that you're blended with. For example, if you're blending with a part that fawns, remind yourself that you also have a part that gets enraged. Once you have a sense of two different parts, you'll have stepped back far enough to realize that you have a Self that is neither fawning nor enraged.

- Keep in mind that it's the Self that can reparent your inner child. You know when you're in Self, or have enough Self-energy, when you can access qualities such as compassion, curiosity, calm, courage, confidence, creativity, and connectedness. Unblending gets easier when you have practices that help you have Self-energy more often. (We'll discuss Self-energy practices at the end of this chapter.)

- When a relational conflict arises, remember that you can speak *for* a part rather than *from* it. Unblend first so you can listen to the feelings and needs of a part. Then you're free to express the feelings and needs to the other person in a clear and confident Self-led way.

- Try to get into the habit of checking in on your parts regularly, the way a healthy parent would. If you ask your parts how they are doing and whether they need anything, they're more likely to feel cared for and to trust you enough to unblend when asked.

As you start to get into the habit of noticing blending and working on unblending, keep in mind that compassion is vital for healing. You unblend so you can feel regulated and are able to offer compassion to a part, not so you can get rid of it. All parts, including ones that seem to sabotage goals, are welcome in IFS. (Don't worry, you'll learn how to work with these parts in the next chapter.)

On your reparenting journey, you'll probably come to see this welcoming, compassionate attitude isn't compatible with some traditional manifestation ideas—in particular, the idea that we have a "victim mentality." I'd love to offer you a different perspective. Let's do a little myth busting, shall we?

Manifestation Myth Busting: "Victim Mentality"

There is a myth going around in manifestation circles that goes something like this: You are not a victim; you just have a victim mentality. You might have even heard this condemnation from privileged influencers on social media in reference to people who were born into poverty and have experienced one form of adversity after another. From a trauma-informed perspective, victim mentality is a shaming way to talk about the real experience of victimhood. Being a trauma survivor is not a chosen state of mind, and criticizing, bullying, and victim-blaming only serve to compound trauma.

The truth is that when you identify with feelings of helplessness, it's because you're either blended with a wounded inner child part and feel dysregulated (this could be chronic) or you're experiencing a current context of trauma. For example, you might be experiencing racial trauma, poverty trauma, migrant trauma, cissexism, ableism, and any other context of potential trauma. What's needed here is compassion, understanding, and real support in order to acknowledge and move through normal feelings of helplessness.

Helplessness occurs when your actions don't lead to the outcomes you want. There are many reasons, including systemic ones, where overcoming obstacles requires more than just an individual effort and a manifesting vision. Community is vital. When you feel the support of a caring community, it's easier to fight for justice and to experience empowerment. Sadly, this isn't always the case, and sometimes you have to look for a new community or chosen family to find support. In addition to outside support, when your wounded inner child feels seen and reparented by you and you know how to upregulate your nervous system so you're not stuck in a dorsal vagal state, it's much easier to feel resourced and empowered. In other words, rather than taking on the toxicity of shame for having a "victim mentality," ask your inner child what they need to feel supported by you.

Now that you understand the importance of having compassion for all of your parts, let's explore some of the common pitfalls of inner child healing.

Common Pitfalls of Inner Child Healing

Inner child healing can backfire as a result of some common issues. Let's look at the most problematic ones and ways to prevent or mitigate them.

Rushing healing. Building a relationship to your inner child is a slow, gentle long-term process. Don't try to force too much vulnerability too soon. You don't want to experience backlash by putting your firefighter parts in a position where they have to push down pain. Take your time and apologize to your protectors if you've unintentionally triggered a wounded inner child part.

Not respecting protectors. If you're having trouble finding compassion for a younger part, it could be because a protector part is activated. If that's the case, it's best to work with and show compassion for protectors. Respect the roles of your protectors and don't try to bypass them or have any hidden agendas. They're just as important as vulnerable parts, and you don't want to favor some parts over others.

Trying to reprocess traumatic memories on your own. It's important to note that the emphasis in reparenting as it's presented in this book is not about recovering memories and reprocessing what happened in the past; it's about cultivating a compassionate relationship with your parts now. Can you help them feel seen, safe, and soothed? Trying to reprocess traumatic memories requires getting the consent of your protectors and additional skills and support. If you'd like to work with the traumatic memories that wounded inner child parts hold, I recommend finding an IFS therapist who can safely guide you through a more comprehensive process.

Expecting your inner child to immediately trust you. You might discover that some of your inner child parts don't immediately warm up to you. That's not unusual. After all, they've been neglected and don't fully trust you yet. Nurturing, protection, and reliability are the keys to earning trust. You might need to repair the relationship by apologizing to a younger part for not listening to it in the past.

As you begin to reparent and keep these pitfalls in mind, you'll start to feel more empowered. You'll also notice that some of your yearnings shift. Maybe your yearning to be seen by trying to manifest success won't be as urgent or anxiety-filled anymore. Maybe your yearning to be saved by manifesting a huge financial windfall won't be as loud because you feel more confident about tackling financial problems. Maybe you'll feel more fulfilled and genuinely grateful. Maybe you'll feel less tied to wound-based goals and wonder what's next.

Exploring what your Self might want you to manifest is often a welcome adventure after years of striving to manifest wound-based goals. Perhaps your Self has more value-based goals in mind, or perhaps it just wants to help you find easier ways to achieve the goals you already have. Either way, when your inner child feels cared for, it will no longer feel desperate and grasp at goals because it feels nurtured from the inside. The stress of trying to manifest from your various parts will no longer consume you. That's when your Self can take over and help you transform how and what you manifest.

Explore What Your Self Wants You to Manifest

Eckhart Tolle has shared that, "Manifestation can only be satisfying and truly effective when it arises out of the Being state of consciousness."[49] This rings true on so many levels. After all, your Self is your Being state of consciousness, and it is connected to the creative intelligence of the Universe. It knows what is best for you and how to get it. You might even be surprised to find that its plans are grander than your own.

According to Dr. Dick Schwartz, "In addition to connecting to neglected parts, as you access more Self you shift from being led by your parts' desires to being led by your heart's desires. That is, you begin getting inklings of a different vision for your life's journey that brings more meaning to it."[50] Schwartz stresses that it's important to allow this vision to emerge naturally from the Self rather than from a manager part. By waiting until your protectors relax and step back, you can "receive your vision rather than create it."[51] Allowing a vision to emerge is consistent with stepping into the allowing energy you learned about earlier. Allowing is open and receptive. Allowing energy happens naturally when you experience Self-energy running through your body.

So, how exactly do you allow a vision to emerge? You practice unblending from your parts so you can get more access to Self. You can also tap into Self-energy through writing, meditating, dancing, singing, painting, and many other creative endeavors. You can feel it when you're in nature. You can access it whenever your nervous system is in a ventral vagal state. You know you're in Self because it's a good feeling in your body. You're openhearted, and your energy is flowing. You feel safe and present. It's when you embody the eight Cs or qualities of Self: creativity, curiosity, compassion, calm, connectedness, confidence, courage, and clarity.

The more often you access Self-energy, the easier it will be to imagine new possibilities for your life. And yet, even as you create space to allow Self-led goals to emerge, inner conflicts will still show up as protectors doubt your vision or pull you in different directions. In the next chapter, you'll learn tools for resolving goal-related inner conflicts.

Take-Home Points

- Your wounded inner child yearns for things that might not be good for you.

- Unblending from your parts is a helpful reparenting tool.

- Reparenting your inner child allows you to release your wound-based goals.

- Self-led goals emerge on their own when you spend more time in Self.

CHAPTER 7

Resolve Goal-Related Inner Conflicts

When you give up struggle, there's a kind of love.

—Joyce Carol Oates, *I Am No One You Know*

You might think that you want the success, money, love, health, and happiness you dream about, but the truth is that there are probably parts of your psyche that desire those things and parts that intentionally block them. For example, some of your parts might not be on board with your goal of exercising early in the morning. Maybe it's because hitting the snooze button for the hundredth time prevents you from succumbing to hustle culture, or maybe it's because hiding your body shields you from unwanted attention when you have a history of sexual abuse. There are many other possibilities, but what each of these parts believes is that working out or getting fit puts you in jeopardy somehow. And they're ready to step in and prevent that from happening. It's not self-sabotage, it's self-protection.

To further illustrate the role of self-protection in manifesting, let's imagine a young man named David. He grew up with two exceptionally successful parents who had high expectations for him. As a child, he felt as though he was under constant scrutiny and worried about disappointing his parents. Over time, he developed a wounded inner child part that felt inadequate. To protect this inner child, two protective parts emerged.

An overachiever part developed that pushed him to excel, and a procrastinator part took over when an important task triggered his fear of failure. The overachiever part wanted to prove David's worth and meet his goal of attending a top graduate program for engineering, but his procrastinator part swooped in and froze him when he was stressed by inadequacy fears, keeping him from doing his best work and sometimes even meeting important deadlines. If he didn't address this inner conflict, it could easily block him from achieving his goal.

David was stuck in what psychologists call a *double bind*. It's when you receive two conflicting messages and are confronted with irreconcilable demands. One part of David wanted to work hard to prove his worth, and one part wanted to prevent feelings of worthlessness by not risking failure. It's a no-win situation. The paradox is that the wound that motivated him also paralyzed him. As a result of these conflicting demands, David's career goals could stall. In IFS, this type of inner conflict is called *polarization*. It's when your parts participate in a tug-of-war and keep you stuck.

Can you think of a goal you have that isn't progressing as quickly or easily as you'd like? If so, is there a part of you that has an agenda, and another part, perhaps an equally vocal one, that wants you to do the exact opposite? Getting to know your parts and how they interact is the inner work necessary to see your blind spots and manifest the things you want in life, no matter what kind of goals you have.

To start, let's look at some common protector parts and how they fit into your personal manifesting type from chapter 3: daydreamer, hustler, and complex manifestor. (We won't include the self-healer type here since it's more aligned with Self-led, value-based goals.) Keep in mind that these lists aren't exhaustive, and the role-based names are for illustrative purposes only. When your parts learn to trust you, you'll find that their names change as they evolve into less extreme roles.

Common Parts and What They Do for You

Let's meet some common protectors that might show up when you're trying to manifest goals. They're split up into the three manifestor types, but you might find that you have parts from all three categories. As you explore which parts you resonate with the most, keep compassion in mind. Although your parts use defense mechanisms that might interfere with manifesting important goals, they're trying to keep you safe. Later in this chapter, you'll learn tools for working with them. For now, identifying your parts will help you become more aware of them, making it easier to unblend.

Daydreamer Manifestor Type Parts

Daydreamer parts are trying to manage nervous system dysregulation that leans toward dorsal vagal activation. They tend to freeze and fawn, and their strategies are more internal and passive.

The spiritual bypasser. This part uses spirituality to protect you from painful emotions. It urges you to have compassion for people who harm you but doesn't help you hold them accountable. It encourages you to forgive prematurely and to engage in toxic positivity. It uses spiritual beliefs and practices to keep your wounds buried rather than heal them. When it comes to manifesting, this part might make you more susceptible to oppressive teachings that don't take trauma or systemic barriers into consideration.

The Self-like part. This part's role is to make it look like you're in Self. It wants you to feel valuable and lovable by making you act like a good person. It might learn a spiritual or healing model, such as IFS, and make you express some qualities of Self. Unlike Self, however, it has a hidden agenda. For example, it might make you extend compassion not for its own sake, but because it wants you to get recognition for being compassionate.

The daydreamer. This part protects you from feelings of helplessness and hopelessness by making you fantasize about your ideal life. If you have this part, you might have a very active internal world, but feel passive or experience disempowerment in your external world. In your fantasies, you have a sense of agency and can have what you want without making changes or overcoming obstacles in the real world. For example, rather than working on relationship issues, you might escape into an elaborate fantasy world where you have a "perfect" partner.

The magical thinker. This part protects you from feelings of helplessness by making you believe that you can control the outside world with your thoughts. For example, this part can make you think you can change the weather by wishing for sunshine. While there's a little magical thinking in manifestation and spirituality, this part uses magical thinking to counteract feelings of anxiety or powerlessness. In its extreme form, magical thinking can also be a symptom of psychological disorders.

The procrastinator. The procrastinator tries to protect you from distressing emotions by making you avoid the source of your stress. In the moment, it doesn't care that putting off a task usually increases the stress. It only wants to put a stop to the emotional discomfort you're currently experiencing by distancing you from the problem. This part affects manifesting when putting off a goal causes you to miss an opportunity because of a deadline or to fail at something because of lack of preparation.

The isolator. The isolator doesn't want you to depend on anyone else because doing so was disappointing or unsafe in the past. It makes you withdraw, either physically or emotionally, to protect you from being vulnerable to criticism, boundary violations, abuse, rejection, and abandonment. This part can affect manifesting by interfering with romantic relationships or making it difficult to form partnerships with people who could potentially assist you in achieving your goals.

The burned-out part. This part tries to keep you from pushing forward when there's a high risk of becoming emotionally or physically depleted. It doesn't see any hope of your situation improving with more effort, so it puts the breaks on all activities. It takes your motivation away and leaves you feeling empty and exhausted. When this part is activated, you usually feel unwell and struggle to cope with everyday tasks, let alone important life goals.

The people pleaser. Fawning is a clear sign that you have an active people pleaser part. Fawning is an adaptive response to threat. It makes you focus on disarming another person so they don't direct harm your way. This can look like trying to make people happy or deferring to others to avoid conflict. If you have this part, you might hide your needs, feelings, and preferences while secretly resenting others. When it comes to manifesting, this part keeps you stuck in unhealthy relationship dynamics that require you to suppress your own desires.

The caretaker. This part's role is to take care of other people so they don't abandon you. It might make you self-sacrifice until you feel like a martyr. If you have this part, you might feel resentful of others and simultaneously feel terrified of not being needed. In its extreme form, this part can make you feel excessively responsible for someone else's behavior and well-being. This is the essence of codependency. Rather than pursuing your own goals, you focus on how other people are doing.

The underachiever. The underachiever has the potential for success but doesn't make an effort because of fear. It's usually afraid of feeling shame for disappointing others. For example, you might have been told that you're gifted throughout your childhood, and now you're afraid of taking on challenges that could lead to failure and doubt about your giftedness. The underachiever might also discourage ambition in order to protect you from unhealthy relationship dynamics. For example, you might have a fear of success because a parent or sibling responded to your earlier successes with envy, contempt, or exploitation.

The pessimist. The pessimist's job is to protect you from disappointment or a deep depression that arises from feeling defeated. By making you think that a goal won't work out, you're less likely to pursue it with high expectations or enthusiasm. Unfortunately, it can be a self-fulfilling prophecy.

The overthinker. This part keeps you in your head, where things are safe, by looking at things from all angles. It believes that thinking harder and longer protects you from taking the wrong action. Unfortunately, rather than problem solving, overthinking usually leads to second-guessing yourself and a state of "analysis paralysis." It affects manifesting by keeping you from taking decisive action.

The intellectual. You probably have this part if you prefer to understand something intellectually rather than emotionally or experientially. This part lives in the world of ideas, where things are safe. It protects you by giving you the sense that learning about Rome is the same as, or almost as good as, visiting it. The intellectual can affect manifesting by making you study or talk about your desires rather than live them.

The wallflower. The wallflower's job is to keep you out of the limelight because attention has been threatening in some way in the past. It might be trying to protect you from criticism, embarrassment, physical harm, envy, or exploitation. There are many reasons for this part to develop; one common reason is having a narcissistic parent who competed with you, used your appearance or achievements to garner attention, bullied you for being more sensitive than them, or embarrassed you in public with their behavior. This part affects manifesting by keeping you from pursuing goals that require being in the spotlight.

The health inhibitor. This part's job is to create physical symptoms in order to get your needs met. It communicates indirectly through the body to get your attention or the attention of others. It also uses symptoms to protect you from behaviors or situations it believes are threatening. Some examples include exhaustion, migraines, and stomachaches. It affects manifesting by making you sick so you don't have to face a challenging goal. For example, you might get a migraine that forces you to cancel a first date. The health inhibitor can also play a role, alongside biological factors, in health outcomes when you're trying to treat a physical ailment.

Hustler Manifestor Type Parts

Hustler parts try to manage nervous system dysregulation in the form of sympathetic activation. They're always on the go and like to exert a sense of control. They tend toward fight or flight, and their strategies are more external and active.

The inner critic. This is a fight stress response in action. The inner critic's job is to attack you when it thinks you're doing something that jeopardizes how people see you. It wants to make you lovable by trying to get you to hide your flaws and constantly improve. Some of your other parts are probably scared of the inner critic or polarized with it, but it's important to see that this part still has a positive intention: it's trying to get your emotional need to be loved met. The inner critic can affect manifesting when it uses criticism to motivate you. Doing so is all about making you fear failure, which often results in you avoiding challenges that might result in failure. Knowing that the inner critic's attacks are waiting for you after setbacks can make you shy away from goals and their inherent obstacles. Despite its intention to help, the inner critic doesn't realize that the willingness to fail is often necessary for success.

The perfectionist. The perfectionist wants to protect you from feelings of worthlessness. Driven by a need for control and a fear of failure, it makes you detail-oriented and devoted to work. It is highly critical and makes you focus on flaws. This part tends to set lofty goals and puts a lot of pressure on you to achieve them. This can lead to controlling behaviors and depression when results are less than perfect or goals go unmet.

The appearance manager. This part tries to make you look attractive in order to be seen and loved. It protects you from disapproval through self-criticism. The appearance manager makes you focus on your looks and engage in constant physical self-improvement. When it comes to manifesting, it might make you overfocus on weight loss goals and put you at risk for developing an eating disorder.

The worrier. This part tries to protect you from potential threats by making you think about only negative outcomes. It doesn't feel safe with uncertainty or lack of predictability. To create a sense of control, it engages in endless what-ifs. When it comes to manifesting, the worrier can make you struggle with decisions because it doesn't want to make the wrong ones. It can also make you ruminate about your dream not coming true. And, if you follow popular manifestation advice, it can make you fear that your negative thoughts will cause negative circumstances via the Law of Attraction.

The overachiever. The overachiever believes it can protect you or get your emotional needs met by making you accomplish goals. Underneath it, you'll usually find a wounded inner child that wasn't emotionally supported and, as a result, never felt good enough or worthy of love. If you are never satisfied with your success and compulsively strive to accomplish more, you might have this part.

The productivity manager. The productivity manager tries to protect you from collapsing into helplessness or feelings of worthlessness. It wants you to spend every second of the day being productive or trying to get ahead. This part urges you to master habits and life hacks. If you feel extreme guilt or anxiety while resting, it's a sign that you might have this part. The productivity manager affects manifesting by making you take so much action that you don't have time to reflect on why you're prioritizing some goals over others.

The know-it-all. This part uses information to protect you from feelings of shame related to helplessness. It wants to be right in every situation and has high standards. It can be unrelenting in offering opinions and advice, and combative when questioned. When it comes to manifesting, this part can make you focus on one solution to the exclusion of more creative, collaborative, or effective ones.

The controller. The controller tries to keep you safe by making everything around you predictable. It fears the unknown or unmanageable and tries to micromanage people, situations, and even a Higher Power. It doesn't like to leave anything to chance and will use manipulation and criticism when it feels like it's losing control. If you have this part, you might be very rigid about how things should go and struggle with letting things unfold during the manifestation process.

The dominator. This part tries to protect you from feeling vulnerable by seeking power. It becomes critical when you feel vulnerable or when it sees vulnerability in others. The dominator tends to interrupt, coerce, and control. You might have this part if you pursue goals at the expense of other people.

The competitor. The competitor tries to protect you from a wounded inner child's feelings of low self-worth. It sees people as either superior or inferior. It has a hard time collaborating with others and keeps score as a way to prove their value or contribution. This part can affect manifesting by making you focus more on how you measure up to others rather than on your goal.

Complex Manifestor Type Parts

If you resonate with the complex manifestor type, you can have any of the parts from the daydreamer and hustler lists as well as some of the following parts. These parts tend to be more extreme firefighter parts. They try to help you manage intense nervous system dysregulation.

The rebel. The rebel tries to keep you safe from anything it sees as potential coercive control. It uses opposition to maintain autonomy and agency. Extreme versions of this part can include criminal behavior (although the rebel is not the only part that might engage in criminal behavior). For example, if you felt controlled by an intrusive parent as a child, you might rebel later by shoplifting from big businesses. This part affects manifesting by making you take impulsive actions that hinder your goals when you feel like your independence or right to choose is being taken away. It might try to rebel against any goals or goal-related plans it thinks are too structured or confining.

The indulger. This part tries to protect you from uncomfortable emotions by encouraging you to seek pleasurable activities. For example, it might make you eat sweets whenever you feel stressed at work. While it seems like the pleasurable activity is a treat or respite from daily stress, it can quickly become a habit. The indulger can affect manifesting by making you engage in activities that offer short-term soothing but have potential consequences for your goals.

The addict. This part uses anything from alcohol to work to keep you from feeling deeply buried emotional pain that's been triggered. The addict is more extreme than the indulger and often has far greater consequences. If you have an overpowering compulsion that negatively impacts your life, it can be a sign that you have this part. The addict affects manifesting by creating obstacles to your goals in the form of financial problems, relationship difficulties, and health issues. While it has a large impact on your life, it's important to remember that this part has a positive intention: to keep you from feeling the pain of the past.

The distractor. Although any of the manifestor types can engage in distractions, this is a more extreme version. It makes it hard to focus on anything that triggers emotional discomfort or pain. The distractor can impact manifesting when your goal requires sustained attention and focus.

The dissociating part. This part numbs your body and makes it hard to think or express yourself verbally. It tries to protect you from the pain of a wounded inner child that has been triggered or the extreme reactions of other parts. The stress of pursuing your goals can trigger dissociation that impacts manifesting. For example, you might struggle to manifest your desired relationship or career opportunity if you zone out and can't communicate clearly during dates or job interviews.

The bridge burner. You might have this part if you have a pattern of ending relationships abruptly and intensely. The bridge burner cuts off connection to avoid being disappointed or abandoned. It struggles with holding two opposing ideas and tends to see things as all good or all bad. This leads to idealizing people and then devaluing and leaving them in a dramatic way. The bridge burner can impact manifesting by ending promising relationships too quickly or turning collaborators into enemies.

Now that you've looked at some of the parts that might come up while you're trying to manifest goals, you can start keeping track of these parts in a journal. Here are some questions you can ask the parts you discover.

Explore Your Parts

Use a journal to identify and keep track of your parts. You don't have to do this activity all at once. Just write down a part whenever you notice it. By doing so, you'll have an easier time spotting when a part is activated, unblending from it, and learning how to lead from Self. Here are some questions to get to know your *protector* parts.

- Where is this part located in your body?

- What does it look like? (Just write down whatever image comes to mind.)

Ask the part these questions directly and just see what answers pop up.

- What do you do for me? What is your job?

- What are you afraid would happen if you didn't do this job?

- What situations or people activate you?

- How do you make me behave?

- How old are you?

Think of the goal you've been working on and ask the part the following questions.

- Do you try to keep me from reaching this goal?

- If so, why is keeping me from it important to you?

- What are you afraid will happen if I reach this goal?

- Are you worried that another part will take over if you don't keep me from it? If so, which part? (This is a sign of polarization. You'll do an exercise later to work with it.)

- How old do you think I am? (Keep in mind that parts have access to only some information and that updating them can be extremely useful. Be sure to update the part with your current age, abilities, and resources. Make a note of how this part responds to your age. It might be surprised by how old and capable you are now.)

Once you're done, thank the part for sharing helpful information with you.

Now that you've explored some of your parts, let's look at which parts tend to get polarized and block you from achieving your goals. Then you'll learn a technique to depolarize them and unblock your goals.

Common Goal-Related Inner Conflicts

Some of your inner conflicts are probably obvious to you. In today's stress-filled culture, it's not unusual to have a productivity manager part that tries to keep you from falling behind and a burned-out part that resents the endless tasks and activities required to keep up. Here are just a few of the other common polarizations that might be keeping you stuck. As you can imagine, the combinations are endless.

The perfectionist and the procrastinator. One part wants everything to be flawless, and the other avoids and delays tasks because it is afraid of making mistakes.

The overachiever and the wallflower. One part wants to accomplish big goals, and the other part avoids any activity that involves being seen or getting attention.

The controller and the rebel. One part tries to micromanage every aspect of manifesting, and the other part doesn't want to be trapped by a goal, so it jumps in to undo everything, often once you're close to achieving the goal.

The people pleaser and the bridge burner. One part tries to please people, and the other part resents not getting its needs met. Eventually the bridge burner puts an end to relationships rather than communicate its needs or manage boundaries in a healthy way.

The overachiever and the indulger. One part works on goals compulsively, and the other gets tired of not having any fun. It then takes over and tries to overcompensate by seeking high levels of pleasure (often requiring a recovery period). This can result in a "work hard, play hard" lifestyle that might not reflect your core values and eventually leads to burnout.

The addict and the inner critic. The addict tries to keep emotional pain from overwhelming you by engaging in addictive behaviors, and the inner critic attacks it with shame. This pattern can make it difficult for you to give your goals the attention they need.

Now that you've started thinking about some of your inner conflicts, you're probably wondering how it's possible to get unstuck and unblock your goals. Your inner critic has probably tried to shame your other parts into cooperating, but that rarely works long term. (Not to mention, it's not exactly self-compassionate!) Let's talk about the process of getting unstuck.

How to Resolve Goal-Related Inner Conflicts

It's time to get unstuck and unblock your goals. In IFS, this is called *depolarization.*[52] It's when you compassionately work with two conflicted parts and help them negotiate a compromise. To get started, let's use a legal metaphor. Your role in resolving conflicts is not that of a judge. You don't listen to both sides and then make a ruling to decide which party (or, in this case, part) wins. Your role is to be a mediator. A mediator is someone who listens to both sides neutrally and helps both parties come to a mutual agreement. Remember that your protector parts are stuck in their roles because they needed to help you survive. Stay compassionate and curious and don't take sides as you help them negotiate. Ask the parts to come up with a compromise so that no one will take over.

Let me give you a quick example of what this might look like. Let's say you have an overachiever part and an indulger part conflict that results in a "work hard, play hard" lifestyle. You invite them to negotiate and let them know that each of their concerns will be heard. The overachiever says it's afraid of becoming overindulgent and losing motivation, and the indulger is afraid of not having any breaks and burning out. You ask them to come up with a compromise, and offer suggestions as needed. Once they come together, they decide that the right compromise is to stop work at seven and watch one episode of your favorite show every day. It's a simple solution. Here's the hard part: You have to follow through. Set a reminder and execute, because this is what it will take to help these parts get unstuck. (Of course, use common sense and don't agree to a compromise that is more harmful than the original conflict.) You can always check on the two parts and see how the compromise is going. Keep working with the parts until you're no longer stuck.

Now that you've worked on resolving inner conflicts, it's time to step into a new future. In the next chapter, you'll learn how to act on your dreams with confidence.

Take-Home Points

- Your protector parts are working hard to keep you safe.

- Some of your protectors have opposing goals that keep you stuck.

- Rather than taking sides, you can accomplish more by asking two polarized parts to come up with a compromise.

- Make sure you follow through with the negotiated compromise.

CHAPTER 8

Act to Support Your Goals Without Chasing Them

Move within, but don't move the way fear makes you move.

—Rumi

Doing the internal work to heal is necessary for releasing blocks, but alone it is not enough to manifest the future you desire. Action is still necessary. Here's the secret though: You only need to take *enough* action. I am a big believer in practicing economy of effort. Take the right amount of action, and no more. Seriously. Manifesting your goals does not have to involve force. You won't ever have to chase the things that are aligned with your Self. In fact, the more Self-energy you have, the more good things come into your life naturally. Sometimes you get into the flow and it feels like, for a time at least, success chases you.

In Taoism, this type of nonstriving is called *wu wei*. It essentially translates to effortless action. It's when you act without force and in harmony with the Universe. This is when you have the most power and can manifest easily and, sometimes, very quickly. It's the difference between manifesting from your wounded inner child parts or protectors and manifesting from Self. Self feels confident and doesn't get attached to outcomes. As you embody more Self-energy, your nervous system is regulated, and you aren't afraid of losing the thing you're trying to manifest. There's no survival energy or desperation in your actions. You're not fueled by dysregulation or the fear of further wounding and dysregulation.

This elevates the purpose of manifesting from a way to fill an unmet need to a way to express your Divinity. You can move mountains more easily when the energy of Self propels your goals.

This is not to say that you can sit back and become passive or that constant action will never be necessary. There will be seasons in your life where a great deal of motion will be required of you. For example, if you just had a baby, your life will be filled with constant little actions. The same goes for starting a business. You'll wear many hats and have to take a million little actions. Even in these seasons though, the energy behind your actions matters. You can take the actions with an attitude of acceptance of your current circumstance and do your best to give yourself compassion, ask for support, and regulate your nervous system. Or you can resent the present moment and fight it the whole time. Neither will be easy, but one will be a lot less painful. The key is still to take action without force.

Using force and overstriving come from feelings of powerlessness. The more Self-energy you embody, the more powerful you feel. And yet, I know how difficult it can be to embody power when your inner child is screaming that it wants—no, *needs*—something desperately. When you're attached to an outcome, it's a big sign that you're blended with a wounded inner child and need to unblend and soothe it. Otherwise, your actions will have so much survival energy attached to them that it will become harder and harder to loosen your grip. This is when it's time to stop and step back. Anytime you're grasping, chasing, pushing, or forcing, it's time to regulate and reparent. This also applies to moments when you feel so paralyzed with fear that you can't take any action. It's time to stop what you're trying to accomplish and regulate and reparent.

Let me give you a personal example. I've experienced both paralysis—*hello, binge-watching shows instead of working on a goal I say I want*—and overstriving. I've also experienced Self-led confidence that guided me straight to my goals with zero resistance. In fact, I keep a list of my experiences with overstriving. It's a reminder that once I let go of forcing or chasing something that is not for me, the perfect thing *always* flows into my life. The moment I release my attachment to the wrong thing, the perfect solution or manifestation shows up like clockwork. Perhaps you've experienced this as well. Your wounded inner child parts and your protectors chase, but your Self simply is. This type of presence is attractive and allowing. Sometimes, the flood gates open, and multiple dreams come true the moment you surrender to the Self. (Don't worry, we'll talk more about surrender in this chapter and how to get there.)

The problem with overstriving is that it rarely works. Force usually meets counterforce and creates resistance. When this happens, the harder you try, the worse it gets. Overstriving can look like:

- Chasing a crush or an ex even though they're not interested

- Trying to change a partner into someone who is a good match for you

- Idealizing a college, company, or job while ignoring better matches for you

- Going after a job or person who looks good on paper, but isn't aligned with your values or long-term goals

- Bidding on a house even though your intuition says it's the wrong house for you

- Using aggressive sales tactics or pitches that repel others

- Trying too hard to make a good impression rather than showing up as yourself and accepting the results

- Giving too much to others hoping that one day it will be reciprocated

- Not respecting other people's boundaries

- Ignoring red flags and barriers that try to lead you in a better direction

- Not moving on from a strategy that isn't working.

If you're on the right track toward your goal, you'll encounter obstacles, but they'll eventually start to dissolve. If they continue to be a struggle or things get worse, it's often a sign that there's a better match for you or a better way to accomplish your goal. Whatever is happening might be a helpful stepping stone to your goal, but it is likely not a good fit. Pushing, forcing, grasping, and chasing won't help. To dispel the illusion that over-striving works, let's make a list of the things you've chased and tried to force.

Your History of Overstriving

Use a journal to complete this exercise or download the worksheet on the website for this book, http://www.newharbinger.com/53042. You'll be looking at how things often work out when you stop chasing and forcing things that aren't good for you.

1. Draw a vertical line down the middle of the page.

2. Number the left side from 1 to 5.

3. Think of something you chased or tried to force that didn't work out. Maybe it was a college acceptance, a job, a home, or a relationship you desperately desired. Write these down on the left side next to the numbers.

4. Now think of what you got in place of the disappointment. Maybe it was an acceptance to a different college where you met your partner. Or maybe it was a job with a better work culture. Perhaps it was a relationship with someone who treated you better. Write these down on the right side of the vertical line.

5. If you have more than five examples, make a longer list and continue to add to it.

Looking at how things ultimately work out when you stop overstriv-ing makes it a lot easier to accept "rejection" or "failure." Even if you only have one example for now, it's a good start. You can still experiment with this idea throughout the day. Pay attention to the little things that don't work out in your daily life and see how much easier things get when you *pause rather than push.* Ask yourself, "Is there a better way?" Take a few deep, centering breaths and see what you feel inspired to do instead.

The truth is that you deserve better than a life of pushing. You deserve so much more than anything or anyone you have to chase or force. Remember, chasing, pushing, forcing, grasping, and overstriving are not signs that you are unworthy. They are signs that your nervous system and wounded inner child need tending. They're signs that you need to regulate and reparent. Once you feel better, you can think more creatively and effectively. Better strategies come to you without strain. And, perhaps most importantly, you find yourself opening to new possibilities you might have rejected while in a dysregulated state. Let's look at regulating and reparenting a little more closely.

Regulate and Reparent

Being regulated and taking action without force are highly effective, but they still need to be authentic. Pretending you don't care and playing hard to get are not the same as feeling regulated and secure. Many manifestation coaches recommend these types of strategies, but let me tell you, you don't need them. They're unhealthy, and the results you get with them are nothing compared to the fulfilling life you can have when you feel truly regulated and secure.

So, how do you implement regulation and reparenting as you begin to take action on your dreams? First, notice which nervous system state you're in when it comes to your goal. If you're anxious and taking too much action, it's a sign that you're in a sympathetic/hyperaroused state. If you're not taking enough action—you feel paralyzed, overwhelmed, stuck, and you're procrastinating or avoiding—you're probably in a dorsal vagal/hypoaroused state. If you're taking just the right amount of action and feel good, you're in a ventral vagal state. Once you know which state you're in, use strategies from chapter 3 to either downregulate or upregulate.

For example, if you're in a sympathetic state and you're so anxious that you keep texting the person you're dating to get reassurance, this is a good time to put the phone down and go for a walk or splash cold water on your face. If you're having trouble taking any action toward your goal, talk to a supportive friend about it, connect spiritually, or do a very gentle exercise. Once you feel more regulated, you're ready to take a small action toward your goal.

Reparenting is similar to regulating except, rather than helping your body feel safe, you're helping your inner child feel safe. First, notice which part of you feels either anxious or stuck. Next, make sure you unblend from it and hear it out. Then, from a place of Self, reassure or soothe it.

Once you've regulated your nervous system and reparented your inner child, you're ready to take action. One of the best ways to move toward your goals with the least amount of resistance and the highest likelihood of success is to break your big goals down into smaller, more achievable ones. These are called "micro-goals."

Succeed Safely Though Micro-Goals

Micro-goals are basically very small goals. A good rule of thumb is, the bigger the fear, the smaller your goal needs to be. For example, if your big goal is to lose weight, your micro-goal for now might be to replace soda with water. Maybe it needs to be even smaller, such as going for a ten-minute walk twice a week. Whatever the micro-goal is, make sure it's achievable. You want an unthreatening, easy win that doesn't feel like a big change.

Achieving a micro-goal helps your nervous system adjust to change slowly, and it gives your parts a gentle experience that disconfirms their fears. It shows them what's possible in a way they can tolerate. In other words, rather than a shock to your system, achieving micro-goals allows you to succeed safely and sustainably. It keeps you from getting lost in the vastness of your dreams and feeling pressure from them. It's easy to feel like a failure when your dream is still far away. With micro-goals, you can feel like a success on a regular basis.

To create a micro-goal, think about the goal you've been trying to reach and, on a regular basis, ask yourself, "What's the tiniest step I could take toward my goal today?" Once you master that micro-goal, keep creating and achieving new ones until you meet your big goal.

Now that you've started taking small actions and feel relatively safe, let's talk about how you can use your intuition to see which actions are most aligned with your Self.

Take Inspired Action

In manifestation circles, it's believed that you should only take action that's based on intuitive or divine guidance. This is often called *inspired action* or *aligned action*. From an IFS perspective, you could say that it's an action that's aligned with and inspired by your Self. For me, this is one of the most fun aspects of manifesting. If I'm feeling dysregulated, I know it's time to regulate and reparent, and then turn inside for guidance. I'm always amazed by the answers I get when I do so.

Before I learned about IFS, I had a long-time practice of writing to what I called my Higher Self for guidance. I would write it a question and then listen for an answer and write it down. Sometimes I would get an image and write it down as well. I learned quickly that I could get surprisingly specific and accurate information as long as I wasn't tied to only hearing what I wanted to hear. The less attached I was to specific answers, the more intuitive information I would get. And because the information was so accurate, I developed a deep trust in my intuition. Even when the answers seemed random, they would always lead to amazing results. It was only when I decided to go against intuitive guidance that I experienced closed doors or negative consequences. Eventually, I learned to listen to even the tiniest intuitive whisper.

Here is how you can consult with your inner guidance and get your own intuitive answers.

Consult Your Inner Guidance

This exercise is a simple Q & A–style conversation with your internal guidance. First write the letter Q and then your question. Then, write an A and take a few deep breaths with long exhales. Once you feel totally regulated, simply wait for an answer. Don't have any specific expectations. Just write down whatever pops into your mind even if it doesn't make sense. Keep writing until your answer feels complete. If you want more clarity about an image or answer, don't interpret it prematurely. Just ask follow-up questions and jot down the answers. Keep in mind that the less afraid you are of the truth, the more intuitive information you'll get. You can also download a worksheet for this exercise on the website for this book, http://www.newharbinger.com/53042.

Here are a few sample questions to start with:

- What's the next step I can take toward this goal?

- Do I need to change course or try a different strategy?

- Should I keep taking action or pause and reflect?

- What is something I haven't considered about this goal?

- Is there a simpler path to achieving this goal?

- Is there something I need to attend to today that will help me move toward my goal?

- What is blocking me from achieving this goal?

- Is there anything I need to let go of to manifest this goal?

- Am I taking the right amount of action toward the goal?

How did that feel? Did you get some answers you weren't expecting? Did you get some guidance about which actions you need to take? Once you start to develop confidence in your inner guidance, it's easier to take just the right amount of action and no more. But how do you know if you've taken enough action and it's time to hand everything over to the Universe? How do you know when it's time to surrender?

Surrender

By the time Maria came to see me for therapy, she was ripe for surrender. She did everything she could to have a baby and was emotionally, physically, and financially done. She was thirty-nine and tired of the ups and downs of infertility. When I explained the concept of *reproductive trauma* to her, she cried tears of recognition. "That's what it's been like, one big trauma that no one really understands," she told me. Her nervous system was spent. While we worked on processing the trauma and healing her nervous system, Maria said she just wanted the Universe to take over. Since she believed in prayer, I asked her if she wanted to bring this intention to prayer. That night, she told the Universe that she'd reached her human limitations and was handing everything over.

This is the essence of spiritual surrender. It's when you take action and then allow the Universe to step in. In research, spiritual surrender is measured by statements such as, "Did my best and then turned the situation over to God."[53] Sometimes people confuse surrender with inaction. This couldn't be further from the truth. Here are a few problematic approaches that tend to masquerade as spiritual surrender:

- Not engaging in any active problem solving because you're stuck in a dorsal vagal state and feel helpless. In research on the psychology of spirituality, this is referred to as a *deferring coping style*.[54] When you defer to the Universe, it means you don't do much to solve your problems. You relinquish all responsibility and expect the Universe to handle them without any assistance from you. This is different from spiritual surrender, and it's associated with poor mental health outcomes.

- Bargaining and pleading with the Universe to manifest the outcome you want. This is called a *pleading coping style*, and it's associated with poor mental health outcomes.[55]

- Trying to gain control by going through the motions of what you think surrender looks like. This is when your protector parts try to convince you that you've surrendered as a strategy to get what they want.

If spiritual surrender isn't something you can do right now, consider adopting a *collaborative coping style* instead. A collaborative approach is when you see the Universe as a partner. In research, it's measured by statements such as, "Tried to put my plans into action together with God."[56] It's when you work together with the Universe to find meaning in difficult situations and generate solutions to problems. This type of approach is associated with positive mental health outcomes.

Another way to think about surrender is that you're not really surrendering to something out there. You're surrendering to your Self, which is always with you and knows exactly what you need. When you surrender to the divine essence inside of you, you act with clarity—trusting that you're led to the perfect solutions at the perfect time. While it can be frustrating to take actions without knowing for certain where they lead, research shows that this type of approach can help you create an inspired life.

Dr. Lisa Miller, professor at Columbia University and author of *The Awakened Brain: The New Science of Spirituality and Our Quest for an Inspired Life*, differentiates between two modes of awareness based on fMRI studies: *achieving awareness* and *awakened awareness*.[57] Achieving awareness is the perspective that you need to control your life. The guiding principle with achieving awareness is getting and keeping what you want. When overused, it changes the brain and is associated with stress, depression, anxiety, and craving. Awakened awareness is the perspective that you are a seeker. Your approach to life isn't about what you can get, but what life wants to show you. It allows you to perceive more choices, opportunities, and connections. You might think you need to only have an awakened awareness and give up all control, but according to Miller, this isn't necessarily practical or possible. In fact, having what she calls a *questing orientation* instead is ideal because it integrates achieving awareness and awakened awareness. With this type of orientation, you can live more fully by being open to what the Universe is showing you and then taking action to achieve it.

But what if you surrender or try to take inspired action only to find that inspiration is leading you elsewhere? What if you start to wonder if *your* plan might not be aligned with the plan your Self or the Universe has in store for you? Then it might be time to assess whether your goal is something you want to keep pursuing.

When Is It Time to Give Up on a Dream?

At some point, you might ask yourself whether you should continue pursuing your dream. Giving up dreams that no longer serve you can free you up to pursue more Self-led, value-based ones. It can also improve your mental health if the dream has been extremely draining. After all, if you're trying to achieve a goal even though it seems like you'll never succeed at it, you're putting yourself at risk for depression. Unreachable goals, such as trying to force your parents or partner to change, keep you stuck and make you feel hopeless. Use the following exercise to assess whether it's time to move on.

Should You Give Up Your Dream?

Your "dream" might be a goal or a very specific way you want a goal to unfold. For example, your dream might be to become an actress, or your dream might be to star in a film with your favorite director. Think about your dream as you answer the following questions in your journal.

- Does this dream have too much power over my self-worth?

- Is this dream serving me?

- Is pursuing this dream costing me my relationships, health, or finances?

- Is this dream achievable, or is pursuing it putting me at risk for depression?

- Is this dream joyful and meaningful to me, or is my wounded inner child trying to get its needs met through it?

- Is this dream a wound-based goal? Will it ultimately limit my ability to experience and express my true, authentic Self?

- What do I think this dream will give me? Can I have any of those things now?

- Is pursuing this dream negatively impacting my mental health?

- What if my mental health continues to decline because of the dream?

- Have I taken enough action to manifest this dream?

- Is this dream urgent?

- Is pursuing this dream making me feel ungrateful for the things that are going well in my life? Is it making me miss the present moment?

- Is pursuing this dream making me miss out on my other dreams?

- Is pursuing this dream making me bitter, or is it helping me be my best self?

- What could I gain from changing, deprioritizing, or letting go of this dream?

- Would I be happier if I accepted things as they are rather than dreamed of a different life?

- Does this dream require a miracle or extreme luck? If so, how long am I willing to wait for it? Are there other ways I could use my energy to manifest good in my life?

If you've reflected on these questions, you might decide that your dream isn't right for you anymore. Grieving is natural when you realize that one of your dreams isn't worth pursuing. Give yourself plenty of compassion and time if that's the case. You might have built your whole identity or lifestyle around this dream, and it won't be easy to change overnight. Once you begin the process of letting it go, keep in mind what you're gaining. Pursuing it might have been hurting you. Can you see how you might heal once you take the energy out of your old dream? Can you do a you-turn and put all of that energy into supporting yourself? Can you give the little one inside of you some love and support so they no longer ache for it? Once you do, you begin the process of making space for something new to come in.

In my experience, Self-led dreams emerge and manifest quickly when we let go of dreams that have been hurting us. We often find ourselves in the flow more of the time, and the Universe seems to support our new goals. Chasing isn't necessary when we're open to things that are good for us. As Eckhart Tolle states in his teachings on conscious manifestation, "If a course of action is in alignment with what the universe wants, it will become empowered."[58]

In the next chapter, you'll learn how to rewire your brain to open to new possibilities.

Take-Home Points

- Overstriving comes from dysregulation and feelings of powerlessness.

- When you feel dysregulated and are overstriving, remember to regulate and reparent.

- Micro-goals help you succeed safely because they allow you to adjust to change gradually.

- Surrender doesn't mean inaction; it means taking action and then letting the Universe step in.

CHAPTER 9

Embrace Positive Emotions for New Possibilities

You have to teach your body emotionally what that future is going to feel like before it happens—and you have to do that in the present moment.

—Dr. Joe Dispenza, *Becoming Supernatural*

In this chapter, you're going to rewire your brain by filling up with positive emotions as you envision new possibilities. Before I explain how this will help you manifest, let's address the elephant in the room. Accessing positive emotions can be tricky for many reasons when you have a history of trauma, including the ones mentioned in chapter 1 on toxic positivity. Joy, gratitude, appreciation, hope, excitement, and positive anticipation aren't easily accessible unless you feel safe. They require being in a ventral vagal nervous system state. You might also have inner child and protector parts that are afraid to feel positive emotions. They also need to feel safe. This is why regulating and reparenting are the first two steps to manifesting if you have a history of trauma.

Consider Jordon. She learned about manifesting from a friend who shared a book with her on the topic. She had a long history of childhood abuse and wanted to find a way to create a more positive future. The techniques seemed to help her friend, who explained that the steps were very simple. She told her, "To become attractive to what you want, all you have to do is forgive everyone and feel grateful for everything." Jordon's heart dropped. She wanted a positive future that included love and success, but just thinking about forgiving her parents and feeling grateful for her childhood experiences felt retraumatizing. Despite strong reservations, she tried to forgive and feel grateful, but her trauma symptoms only got worse. She experienced more flashbacks, dissociation, insomnia, and shame. Jordon decided that if manifesting the future she wanted required more emotional pain, it wasn't possible. She gave up trying to manifest and continued to struggle with old patterns and settling for less than she deserved.

Sadly, many trauma survivors who learn about manifesting try to force themselves to forgive or to feel grateful for their traumas. In spiritual communities, they are often told that this is something they *should* do for many reasons: to clear their energy, to have a higher vibration, to attract good things—you name it. Forgiveness and gratitude are seen as the price of entry to a good life. Before we talk about a healthy, trauma-sensitive version of positive emotions, let's clear this myth up right now.

Manifestation Myth Busting: "You Have to Forgive"

There is a forgiveness practice that's popular in manifestation circles called Ho'oponopono. It's a traditional Hawaiian healing mantra that is believed to release negative experiences. It involves repeatedly stating the following: "I'm sorry. Please forgive me. Thank you. I love you." The idea behind the practice is that it clears the past and makes you take full responsibility for your life. Other popular practices focus on forgiving others for what they did to you. If practices like these help you and you see positive results, by all means, use them. Or if you want to use them to ask your inner child for forgiveness for not tending to it in the past, that's fine too. If not, please don't think it is necessary and that you are hopeless.

Focusing on self-forgiveness can be harmful to trauma survivors because it is likely to increase feelings of self-blame. Trying to force forgiveness, especially forgiving perpetrators without holding them accountable, can be extremely retraumatizing. Rather than releasing the past, these types of practices can exacerbate trauma symptoms or lead to spiritual bypassing. The truth is that forgiveness isn't necessary to heal or to manifest. To heal, focus on regulating your nervous system and reparenting your inner child. By doing so, you can release the energy of the past without forgiveness. (But if forgiveness comes as a result, that's fine too.)

For example, let's say that Jordon learned a trauma-informed approach to healing that included regulating and reparenting. She felt empowered by the possibility of releasing the past and decided that she would be a cycle breaker—the first to put a stop to the passing down of trauma in the family. In the process, she might get in touch with feelings of anger for what happened to little Jordon and grief for the love and protection she didn't receive. Rather than feeling compassion for her abusive family and why they acted the way they did, she would focus on reparenting little Jordon so she feels nurtured and safe. She would start to honor herself by prioritizing her own emotional needs and setting boundaries. By doing so, Jordon could release the intergenerational trauma she carried inside without forgiveness or gratitude. The only relationship she would need to focus on is the one with herself.

Now that you know forgiveness and gratitude aren't required for releasing the past, let's look at how embracing positive emotions in a trauma-sensitive way can help you manifest the future you want.

Using Positive Emotional States to Rewire Your Brain

In previous chapters, you learned how to regulate your nervous system and reparent your inner child. Now you're going to learn the last step to manifesting in a trauma-informed way: rewiring your relationship to your goals. While your body and inner child might feel safer, expecting and believing in positive possibilities can still feel out of reach. After all, if you've experienced trauma, your brain has been wired for hypervigilance, not hope. You look out for and expect the worst to happen, not the best. To reverse this pattern, you'll have to actively teach your brain to open to the possibility that good things are coming. You won't even need to believe that something good *will* happen, just that something good *could* happen. To do that, we're going to link positive emotional states with your goals.

You might recall from science class that neurons that fire together wire together (this is known as Hebb's axiom). Connections in your brain are made when two things happen simultaneously. This is why sensory cues, such as smells, can easily evoke memories. We're going to use this to our advantage to create positive brain connections. To do that, I'm going to offer a simple idea: Try to focus on manifesting your goals only when you're in a regulated state or experiencing a pleasant emotion. For simplification, let's call this a *manifesting mood*.

When you're in a manifesting mood, focus on manifesting. Visualize, look at your vision board, daydream, say affirmations, take inspired action, listen to podcasts on manifesting, and plan for the future. When you're dysregulated and experiencing an unpleasant or challenging emotional state, put manifesting aside. Instead, focus on regulating, reparenting, or simply living your life.

In chapter 2, I introduced the idea of a manifesting mood. I want to clarify here why focusing on manifesting only during this state is so powerful. The reason for this shift in focus is it's hard to be optimistic and hopeful about the future in a dysregulated state. Your prefrontal cortex— your thinking brain—is compromised in a dysregulated state, making it hard to think and plan clearly and rationally. In a "negative" mood, your negativity bias also gets worse, and you're more likely to notice negative things. This is called *mood congruent attentional bias* because the mood you're in helps you perceive things that confirm it more readily. During a "negative" mood, you're also more vulnerable to having negative thoughts and recalling negative memories. This is because it's easier to see through the lens of your current emotion and to retrieve mood-congruent information from memory.

In other words, shifts in mood lead to shifts in thinking. Unpleasant or challenging "negative" moods help you notice the negative, think negatively, and recall painful memories. Positive moods, on the other hand, help you notice the positive, think positively, and recall positive memories. Your emotional state influences what you perceive, think, and remember. This *mood bias* is nothing to be ashamed of, and you don't need to run toward toxic positivity in order to remedy it. You can simply notice when you're experiencing a difficult emotion or dysregulated state and work on regulating or reparenting. But please be kind and gentle with yourself if regulating doesn't always come easily. None of us are regulated all the time. Just keep in mind that when you're in a dysregulated state, your thoughts about manifesting and your future will be negatively skewed. I call this *seeing through the lens of dysregulation.* It's not a reflection of what's possible for you; it's simply a state during which it's hard to believe that good things are coming.

Once you're in a regulated state, it will be easier for you to have supportive thoughts and positive expectations. Your thoughts will naturally be biased toward the positive. During this time, it will be easier for you to believe in your dreams coming true. The following table will help you see each state and how it feels.

Nervous System States and Manifesting Goals

Dysregulated	Regulated, "Manifesting Mood"	Dysregulated
Outside WOT	Inside WOT	Outside WOT
Hyperarousal	Optimal arousal	Hypoarousal
Sympathetic state	Ventral vagal state	Dorsal vagal state
Survive mode	Create and thrive mode	Survive mode
Feel unsafe	Feel safe	Feel unsafe
Anxious, angry	Calm, confident	Hopeless, helpless
Doubt	Belief	Disbelief
Anxious thoughts	Supportive thoughts	Pessimistic thoughts
Too much action	"Just right" amount of action	Not enough action

Dysregulated	Regulated, "Manifesting Mood"	Dysregulated
"There is one path to my goal."	"There are many paths to my goal."	"There are no paths to my goal."
"It's impossible without force."	"It's possible."	"It's impossible."
"I must manifest it."	"I'm okay with or without it."	"I can't manifest it."

By focusing on manifesting only during a manifesting mood, you'll link supportive thoughts and positive expectations with your dreams. Through repetition, you'll rewire your habitual response to your dreams from one of doubt and disbelief to one of hope and possibility. Eventually you'll reach a tipping point where you'll start to expect good things to happen. The result will be confidence and an openness to solutions. After all, when you believe something is possible, you expect solutions to come. This becomes a self-fulfilling prophecy. Your reticular activating system— the part of your brain that scans your environment to determine what's important—will start noticing more opportunities. It will seek out information that matches the things you've been visualizing and expecting.

Next, let's look at trauma-sensitive ways to gently access and build a tolerance for positive emotional states so you can be in a manifesting mood more often.

Glimmers

Glimmers are the opposite of triggers.[59] Triggers are cues that signal danger and activate a stress response. They might be sights, smells, sounds, or symbols that evoke "negative" emotions, dysregulate you, and require coping strategies. Glimmers, on the other hand, signal safety. They are the things in your environment that let you know it's okay to relax because you're safe. Coined by psychotherapist and author Deb Dana, glimmers are micro-moments of ventral vagal energy that make you feel good. In other words, a glimmer is something pleasurable that sparks a feeling of joy, hope, belonging, awe, or genuine gratitude. It can be anything from seeing a rainbow to having a nice cup of coffee, depending on your personal preferences.

Here are a few examples of glimmers:

- A friendly face

- The smell of fresh flowers

- A beautiful sunrise

- Sparkly snowflakes

- A soft blanket

- Sun on your skin

- An act of kindness

To get the mood boosting effect of glimmers, you must actively look for them. Glimmers are subtle and fleeting. We tend not to notice them because we're wired to scan for and attend to threats. This negativity bias is even more pronounced for trauma survivors, making it difficult to see the good. As a result, it's necessary to search for glimmers and pause long enough to take them in. We have to intentionally orient toward pleasurable moments and expand our capacity to hold space for them. Try the following exercise to improve your ability to find and savor glimmers.

Go on a Glimmer Quest[60]

In this exercise, you're going to actively look for glimmers. When you first start, set an achievable number of glimmers to look for. You might want to begin with finding just one glimmer every day. Once you get comfortable with finding glimmers, aim for a higher number.

1. Set an intention to look for glimmers.

2. Keep track of the glimmers you find in your journal. This will help you remember the good that is all around you.

3. Recognize the signs that you've spotted a glimmer. Your body feels relaxed and safe. You feel joyful, connected, appreciative, or hopeful.

4. If you can, savor the glimmer by staying with the feeling for just a few seconds.

5. Later, reflect on the glimmers you experienced. See if there is a pattern to the type of people, places, activities, and things that light you up. Can you have more of these in your life?

Going on a glimmer quest might sound simple, but these small moments of positive emotions are powerful. They can give you hope when you're discouraged or dysregulated and haven't been in a manifesting mood for days. They can even help you expand your WOT by allowing your nervous system to experience safety and joy on a regular basis. Once you develop a practice of tuning in to these micro-moments, you'll begin to anticipate finding glimmers in your day. Before you know it, they will appear everywhere!

Keeping track of your glimmers in a journal is especially helpful because it can provide insight into what feels good to your nervous system. Just make sure your glimmer quests don't become rigid or stale. Allow room for flexibility and variety. For example, if you notice that your favorite park no longer gives you a sense of peace and tranquility, try a different park or maybe a completely different type of activity. To ensure that you have enough opportunities to experience glimmers, make a list of a variety of pleasurable activities and schedule them. It's all too easy to get stuck in a rut and forget to make time for joyful experiences.

Once you master noticing and experiencing micro-moments of positive emotions, you're ready for more expansive ones.

Glows and Expansive Emotions

A *glow* is a deeper or more expansive state of safety and joy.[61] You can turn a glimmer into a glow by staying with it for at least thirty seconds.

Rather than moving on, you can soak it all in—the sensations, the positive emotions, and the thoughts that come up as a result of the glimmer. By sitting with the experience a little longer, you're deliberately internalizing it and making it easier to access positive emotions later. Psychologist Dr. Rick Hanson calls this *taking in the good.*[62] He states that the practice of pausing to feel and allow positive experiences to sink in rewires our brain to overcome our natural negativity bias. The more positive experiences you take in, the harder it will be to ignore them in the future. This is especially true when you intensify a positive experience.

But how do you intensify a positive experience to absorb all the good feelings from it? As I write this, it's early in the morning, and the world is quiet. My black Lab is happily napping at my feet while I sip my favorite coffee and listen to the birds outside. I notice that this is a positive experience—the feeling of aloneness without loneliness. The little joys of sleeping pets and the aroma of French vanilla. I know it's fleeting and that the house will start rumbling with activity soon. I stop to put my hand on my heart and take it all in. My eyes well up as I do this. I feel moved by this seemingly small moment of appreciation. Every time I focus on my heart in this way, it feels like it's opening for the first time. I sit with the feeling as long as I can—only about one minute—and then let it go. Like all feelings, even deeply visceral ones, it's impermanent.

To experience an expansive emotion, you must open to it and feel it in your body for a few seconds. Make it as big and full as you can and marinate in it. Feel it in your heart. Allow yourself, and any inner child parts that need it, to be nourished by the feeling. Absorb the experience and let it become a part of you. Allow every cell in your body to glow with the feeling. To take it a step further, do this with the intention of having more good things in your life.

Staying with feelings this strong isn't always going to be easy, and that's okay. They're peak emotional experiences, not ones you need to sustain. On most days, aim for emotional balance instead. Not every moment has to, or should, have the intensity of a music concert. Get a glimpse, and you'll open to new possibilities. Grasp for them and they'll lose their magic. Experiment with amplifying positive emotional states and then let them go. If "negative" emotions come up alongside them, that's fine too. Just allow room for them to be in the background and focus on the expansive positive emotion.

Over time, you'll notice that you can access and amplify intense positive emotions under certain conditions. Maybe it's through live music, exercise, travel, nature, or thinking about someone or something you love. It's good to become aware of these and to start using them intentionally to create self-induced emotional states. For example, there are three conditions in which I can easily access intense positive emotions.

1. **Driving alone, windows down, blasting my favorite music.** This is a multisensory experience with a feeling of agency and freedom I love. Since music is a powerful mood enhancer that can easily induce and intensify a feeling, sometimes I'll listen to a playlist I created to amplify a specific feeling. (It goes without saying that this requires keeping an eye on safety and speed.)

2. **Looking at an expansive natural vista.** This is usually a spiritual experience for me. I feel a sense of awe and transcendence. In such moments, my own concerns feel small and temporary. Oceans, mountains, or a sky full of stars easily put me in this state. (Studies show that looking at and even smelling nature can boost your mood.[63])

3. **Recalling positive past experiences I've intentionally wired into memory.** I'm not talking about looking through past memories to find good ones. Doing that could easily trigger traumatic memories, especially when you have complex trauma. I'm referring to carefully choosing memories I identified as positive experiences at the time (which I often do by saying, "I want to remember this," while taking them in). (Studies show that recalling happy memories can boost your mood;[64] my trauma-informed modification is to choose uncomplicated positive memories without combing through the past.)

Emotions felt in your heart are particularly potent and good to amplify. Whether you're feeling a loving emotion, such as appreciation or compassion, or taking a positive experience and imagining it fill your heart, it will have an effect on your physical heart. It will release oxytocin—the love hormone—to quickly reduce stress and make you feel good. Research by the HeartMath Institute also demonstrates that positive emotions, such as love and joy, create a more ordered wavelike heart rhythm pattern when looking at heart rate variability, which they refer to as *heart coherence*.[65] In a coherent state, the two branches of your autonomic nervous system—the sympathetic and parasympathetic—are in synch with one another. When you're in an incoherent state, they're out of synch, and your heart rhythm pattern looks erratic and irregular rather than wavelike when plotted on a chart.

Heart coherence is not only important for health and well-being; it's been discussed as a tool for manifesting. According to author Dr. Joe Dispenza, an elevated emotion—one that represents heart coherence—is magnetic, and when it's paired with a clear intention, it changes your energy and has the power to produce your intended effect.[66] I'd like to propose that you try this technique as a psychological experiment. At the very least, combining your clear intention with an expansive, heartfelt emotion will provide you with the physiological and mental health benefits of positive emotions and more optimism. You'll feel good and be more open to possibilities. If you believe in an energetic component to manifesting, you'll also be connecting to and calling in a new potential reality in a very real sense. Either way, you'll be moving in the direction of your goal.

The following exercise is like the desired outcome one you learned in chapter 2. It's a visualization exercise, except this time, you'll be focusing more on the physiological experience of the emotion involved. Visualization is a scientifically proven way to improve performance and success in many areas. Psychologists who study visualization call it *mental rehearsal*. In this exercise, you're going to rehearse in your mind (and body) what it will feel like when you reach your goal, and then you're going to expand the feeling. Afterward, I'll share how I used a variation of this visualization exercise to become pregnant.

Visualizing Your Desired Outcome with Expansive Emotions

1. First, make sure that you're in a manifesting mood. If you're not, regulate or reparent instead and try again later.

2. Get into a comfortable position. Relax your body and close your eyes if you like.

3. Think about your goal and clearly identify the outcome you'd like to experience.

4. Next, identify the feeling you'll have once you achieve the goal. Maybe it's joy, peace, or excitement.

5. In vivid multisensory detail, imagine the outcome as if you're living it. Make the visualization like virtual reality and imagine moving around in the scene. (Don't try to figure out how you'll achieve the goal. Leave room for different possible paths and just focus on the outcome.)

6. Next, focus on the feeling of success. Let it start out as a glimmer—a small positive experience—and then expand it to a glow. Find the posture and breathing that bring a feeling of success. Congratulate yourself. Feel your whole body fill up with and radiate the feeling of success. Allow it to grow, then sit with it for a few seconds.

7. Next, focus on the emotion you identified earlier. How does it feel to achieve your goal? Let the feeling start out as a glimmer and then expand throughout your body. If you can, imagine it opening your heart and nurturing you. Breathe deeply with long exhales. Allow the feeling to fill you up, deepen, and radiate outward. Sit with it for a few seconds and feel yourself glowing.

8. Whenever you're ready, open your eyes and slowly adjust to the room.

How do you feel about your goal after this exercise? I hope it gave you the feeling that what you want is possible. Now that you've got those neurons firing together so they'll wire together, let me tell you about my own experience with visualization.

My Visualization Experience

I have a long history of successfully using visualization to manifest goals. But, as you may recall from the introduction, this came to a halt when I experienced infertility after years of researching it for my dissertation. For a while, I was simply dysregulated. Then, one day, the idea of manifesting moods came to me. I decided that I would only focus on manifesting and pregnancy when I was in a regulated state. This allowed me to enjoy visualizing again. I even created a visualization practice around regulation.

It was the summer before I started a new psychologist position, and I had two months off all to myself. Almost every day, I laid by a pool and visualized. I relaxed my entire body and imagined the sun filling me with healing light. And then I visualized sitting on my couch with one of my dearest friends as she held my baby (this provided the additional element of co-regulation). I imagined it in vivid multisensory detail. The couch, the room, the smiles, the laughter. I let myself feel joy and then expanded the feeling to really wire it in.

When I wasn't in a manifesting mood, I attended to my emotional wellness and turned my focus away from manifesting. I did small, uplifting things for myself to feel a sense of agency and to remind myself that my happiness didn't depend on achieving a goal. After visualizing my friend interact with my baby on my couch for just one month, I got the idea to try a new fertility treatment and became pregnant before the end of the summer. A few months later, my friend was holding my baby on the same couch, just like I imagined.

You might be saying to yourself that visualization doesn't always work so easily, and you'd be right! Visualizing the outcome doesn't always work because there are many steps and obstacles along the way. Even worse, visualizing the outcome can zap you of your motivation to take action.[67]

This is because it tricks your brain into thinking you've already achieved the goal and releases dopamine to make you feel good.

Research shows that it's equally important to visualize—mentally rehearse—how you're going to respond to challenges during the process of manifesting.[68] You have to teach your nervous system to manage stressors that will inevitably come up. For that reason, we're going to do a visualization of how you'll use regulating and reparenting to overcome obstacles to your dreams.

Visualize Yourself Regulating and Reparenting

In this exercise, you're going to imagine yourself regulating your nervous system and reassuring your inner child when working on your dream gets hard and you want to quit. Maybe something you thought was the path to your goal didn't work out and shakes your confidence. Or maybe you don't feel up to working on your goal lately and need a boost of motivation. Pick a scenario that might come up as you work on your goal for this exercise. Maybe a date or job interview didn't go smoothly, or you've been working on a goal but it's still too soon to see results.

1. See yourself hitting the roadblock. You feel discouraged and frustrated. You wonder why you thought this was going to work out in the first place. You start to spiral, and then, in a moment of clarity, you *notice* that you're spiraling downward. You catch yourself. You take a deep breath with a long exhale. You tell yourself that it's time to regulate and reparent.

2. See yourself managing your stress and nervous system arousal. You take a few deep breaths with long exhales. Then, you find and release tension from your body. Next, you stand up and shake off stress for a few seconds. You take a few more deep breaths and sit back down to relax. You put your hand on your heart and connect inside.

3. Next, you decide to soothe and reassure the younger part of you that's worried or discouraged.

4. You unblend and see this younger part as separate from you. You send them compassion. You tell them what they need to hear to feel supported. For example, "I get it, you're worried, but I've got your back. We'll be okay no matter what. I'm right here with you."

5. See the younger part responding well to your nurturing. See them relax and feel soothed and cared for.

6. You start to feel more confident and present. You have the felt sense of confidence, the "I've got this" feeling. You feel more Self-energy coming into your body, and you stand up and take the next right, healthy action toward your goal.

7. Whenever you're ready, open your eyes and orient to the room.

I hope this exercise helps you overcome obstacles. Practice it regularly, and regulating and reparenting will become natural habits. Over time, your confidence in manifesting your goals will increase. Even as that happens, it's good to stay grounded so you don't lose sight of balance and discernment. Next, let's look at what can go wrong when we take confidence too far.

A Little Warning About Too Much Confidence

Opening to positive emotions will trigger an upward spiral and help you believe in possibilities. This is something I want you to aim for with one caveat. Along with encouraging you to dream big, I want to caution you about engaging in excessively risky behaviors with your finances, health, and well-being in the process. Recent research on people who believe in manifesting suggests that they are more likely to become overconfident and take risks that aren't necessarily wise.[69] As you begin to believe in possibilities, it's still important to use discernment.

To protect yourself from becoming vulnerable to poor decision making and exploitation, let's look at some specific things to watch out for when confidence in your ability to manifest increases.

- Get-rich-quick schemes, risky investments, and scammers who exaggerate claims and prey upon your newfound belief in possibility

- "Healers" who try to sell you their "miracle cure" and discourage you from following medical advice

- Narcissists who love-bomb you with excessive flattery ("You're my soulmate") and lofty promises ("I will take care of you and make all your dreams come true")

- Charismatic spiritual teachers, covert cult leaders, and unscrupulous life coaches who love-bomb you with excessive flattery ("You're special") and lofty promises ("I can teach you to be enlightened or rich like me") in order to exploit you financially or sexually

Believing in possibilities doesn't have to come at the expense of your wallet or your heart. You can be open to new opportunities while still using discernment and caution when it comes to anything that seems too good to be true. Evaluate opportunity costs and, whenever possible, take any sense of urgency out of making decisions so you can accurately determine what's good for you. After all, manifesting isn't just about what you get; it's about who you become in the process. You want to become someone who is open and wise—someone who takes healthy risks and plans well for the future. You want to take your future self into consideration when making choices, ensuring that you succeed and thrive.

In the next chapter, you're going to get to know your ideal future self and learn how you can start embodying them now.

Take-Home Points

- You don't have to forgive or feel gratitude for the past to manifest successfully.

- To feel good, look for glimmers and turn them into glows.

- To manifest more successfully, you don't have to believe that good things *will* happen, you only need to be open to possibilities—to believe that good things *could* happen.

- Visualize the outcome as well as the process of overcoming challenges.

CHAPTER 10

Embody Your Future Self Now

Strengthening your connection to your future self can boost your willingness to take more actions on your future self's behalf.

—Hal Hershfield, *Your Future Self*

In previous chapters, we talked about your relationship to past selves and how reparenting them can help you release emotional blocks to manifesting your dreams. Now let's take a look at how your relationship to your future self can help you manifest those dreams. The reality is that most of us imagine a stranger when we think of our future self. And yet, studies show that when we develop an intimate relationship with our future self and care about them, we have better outcomes. It can improve our finances, fitness goals, and mental health.[70] In other words, it can help us manifest the future we desire.

Let's say your goal is to eat healthier so you can have more energy and focus. You've been on a healing journey, and things are going well. You've been regulating your nervous system and reparenting your inner child. You set micro-goals daily so it's easier to feel successful and make changes in a way that feels safe. Things are going well until you host a party and are now home alone with a week's worth of your favorite dessert leftovers. Now you're faced with a choice. Do you find a way to get rid of the food or have a few bites, even though you've seriously struggled with moderating sugar in the past? You rationalize that you can eat some today because you can always go back to healthy foods tomorrow. In other words, you assume that your future self can deal with resisting sugary foods. You imagine that your future self is a stranger—not someone you know well and care about. You decide that they can deal with the consequences of today's food choices. You end up eating a lot more desserts than you intended to. The next day, you forgo your salads and continue to eat the leftovers. By the end of the week, you experience cravings and go to the store to buy more desserts. You've eaten so much sugar that you start experiencing fatigue and brain fog again. Regulating your nervous system and making healthy choices require more effort now. It takes some time, but eventually you manage to reset and get back to eating healthier foods.

If you're like most of us, you've probably experienced setbacks like these. You start out with a goal and then have difficulty sticking to it. Hopefully, with some self-compassion, you're able to bounce back and resume your plan. But what if it were easier to make choices that are aligned with your goals? What if all it took was having a very vivid picture of your future self and feeling empathy for them? Research shows that if you have a close relationship to your future self and can bring this relationship to mind when making a choice, it's easier to bridge the gap between where you are now and where you want to go.[71]

Here's the fun part: The more you think about your future self (while in a manifesting mood), the more positive possibilities you can create for yourself. Thinking about your desired future and making plans to get there is called *pragmatic prospection*, and it's linked to positive outcomes, including higher productivity levels and life satisfaction, and lower levels of depression and anxiety.[72] In this chapter, you'll learn how to create your desired future, make sensible plans to get there, and leave enough room to let the Universe intervene with some magic.

To start, let's get a sense of your desired future self.

Your Desired Future Self

When you're in a manifesting mood, use a journal and complete the following questions to get a vivid image of your future self. Include details, but make sure your vision is open enough so you can see many paths to getting there. This will reduce survival anxiety that might come up when you think there's only one path to getting what you desire.

- What makes your future self light up and feel joy?
- What type of house best suits them?
- What type of friends do they have?
- What clothes do they like?
- Do they manage their finances well?
- How do they manage their health?
- Do they have pets?
- What type of romantic relationship do they have?
- Do they have children?
- Do they like to travel? If so, where do they go?
- What do they do for fun?

How would you act today if this were true? Can you dress as your future self today and do one activity they like? Let's say your future self wears designer clothes, and you can't afford them now—could you make a small purchase at a designer consignment store today? If they are a great cook, could you experiment with one recipe today?

Are you getting a sense of what your future self feels like and how they move in the world? If you're struggling to imagine them, keep in mind that they are an evolved version of you. Let's look at how you create this evolved version.

You Create Your Future Self

Your future self is shaped by your vision, your choices, and your personal growth. It's simply a more mature version of you. You're probably different than you were ten years ago. The same goes for your future self. The reason this might be difficult to accept is that we forget we're always a work in progress. This is called the *end-of-history illusion.* It's the false belief that, despite changing in the past, you won't continue to evolve. The reality is that you will continue to change. If you work on healing through regulating your nervous system, reparenting your inner child, and rewiring your relationship with your goals, you'll grow in positive ways.

You'll eventually notice some of the following changes:

- You'll have an easier time distinguishing between discomfort and danger.

- You'll feel safer and become bolder when it comes to your dreams.

- Your self-worth will increase.

- You'll feel more deserving.

- You'll stop settling for things you accepted in the past.

- You'll be resourceful and creative rather than endure bad situations.

- You'll realize that there are many different paths to your goal.

- You'll be more open to receiving positive things into your life.

To accelerate these changes, let's do an exercise to imagine a future in which you embody more Self-energy.

Bring Self-Energy into Your Future

This exercise will help you imagine a future in which your identity is no longer bound by burdens of the past. You'll connect to your Self and begin to see that your potential is limitless.

1. First, check in to see if you're in a manifesting mood. If not, regulate or reparent first.

2. Relax your body and close your eyes if it feels comfortable to do so.

3. Next, you're going to imagine your future self, except this time, see them as having more Self-energy than you currently embody. Remember the eight Cs? Imagine that your future self is:

    - More confident

    - More curious

    - More connected

    - More calm

    - More clear

    - More compassionate

    - More courageous

    - More creative.

4. Sink into the feeling of being this expansive version of your future self. Sit with the pleasure of being still and centered, knowing you can easily move from an old reality and identity into a new, limitless one.

5. Next, imagine that this future self is coming toward you. They ask for your permission to blend with you so you can embody more of these qualities today. If you consent, imagine their energy harmonizing with yours and filling you up.

6. Thank your future self for helping you live your dream life. Imagine that they care about you and always light a path in front of you to follow.

Hopefully this exercise helps you feel ready to step into a new chapter of your life as your future self. Even as you do, there will be times when it is difficult to imagine that new possibilities are truly available to you. This is where role models can be helpful.

Use Role Models

If you recall my story from the introduction, you'll remember that I was a political refugee who lived in a refugee camp and then grew up in the inner city. The idea of living in an idyllic neighborhood was a big stretch for me. I couldn't even imagine it until I saw it with my own eyes. My best friend moved out of the inner city and into a beautiful neighborhood. For the next few years, I would spend many weekends at her house. We would roam all over the town, and before long, it felt as if I could live there. After all, if she could do it, why couldn't I? From that moment, I believed it was possible.

In psychology, this is called the *Bannister effect*. Seeing someone else do something you thought was impossible helps you break the psychological barrier between you and your goal. The phenomenon is named after Roger Bannister, who was the first to run a mile under four minutes. This was a feat runners previously thought was impossible. After Bannister, the psychological barrier lifted, and many runners quickly followed suit. In the next exercise, you'll use a role model to do the same.

Let Your Role Model Inspire You

Use this role model exercise whenever you're struggling to believe that something you want is possible. (You can also listen to a recording of this exercise at http://www.newharbinger.com/53042.) It will put your doubts on "pause" and give you the confidence to dream bigger.

1. Think of your role model: someone who is living the dream you want and inspires you.

2. Begin by centering and grounding yourself so your nervous system feels regulated.

3. Imagine your role model engaging in the activity or lifestyle you desire. Make your image real by adding details, such as vivid colors, smells, and sounds.

4. Now see your role model extend their hand to you. They're smiling and saying, "It's your turn." They're encouraging you with support and letting you know that they believe in you.

5. You take their hand and step into your own version of the dream life you want.

6. See yourself engaging in the activity or lifestyle with vivid multisensory details.

7. Do this for just a few minutes until it feels complete.

8. Repeat whenever you need a boost of inspiration or courage.

I hope that connecting to your role model has helped you feel like the life you want is possible. Opening yourself to new possibilities can be a stretch for anyone, but it can be especially challenging when you have a history of trauma. Self-protection is understandable, but you can use the protocol you've learned in previous chapters for breaking through psychological barriers. Next, let's review the protocol.

Break Your Own Ceilings

If you bump into a fear or limit, you've probably hit a self-imposed ceiling based on familiar self-protection. That's okay and normal. No need to panic. Just go back to the three Rs you've learned: regulate, reparent, and rewire.

1. Regulate your nervous system so it feels safe.

2. Reparent your inner child parts by making them feel seen, safe, soothed, and heard (this includes resolving conflicts between parts by negotiating agreements).

3. Rewire by focusing on goals only when you're in a manifesting mood.

To break through ceilings and become your future self, it can be beneficial to do a little time traveling into the future and imagine different scenarios. This type of contrasting can help you commit to the future you want and take the necessary steps to get there. In the next activity, you'll look at two different roads you might travel.

Which Road Will You Take?

1. Imagine that it is ten years from now, and you've committed to your vision of your future self. You've been regulating, reparenting, and rewiring. You've given yourself permission to be your best self. You've used your intuition and taken action steps to make your dreams a reality. How do you feel?

2. Now imagine the opposite. It's ten years from now, and you haven't worked on healing. You haven't given yourself permission to be your best self or taken any action steps. How does this feel?

3. Reflect on these two different roads and decide which one you want to take. If it's the first, write down plans to make it happen.

Believe you can have what you want and begin today! The more committed you are to your future self, the faster it turns into reality. Focus on the future self you want and bring them to mind when you are faced with a goal-related decision, such as spending wisely or overspending. Simply ask yourself, "Is this choice aligned with my desired future self?" Keep the image of your future self close and care about them the way you would a loved one.

One way to commit to your ideal future self is to begin acting as if what you want is already a present reality. Next, we'll explore this strategy and see how you can apply it today.

Act As If It's Already True

Big changes can be painful because they're a shock to your nervous system. You can get your nervous system ready for changes by acting as if your desired reality has manifested. This is usually referred to as *acting as if*. It's a manifestation strategy that gives you the *felt sense* of your dream come true. To try it, all you have to do is act as if your desired future is already here. For example, if you're trying to manifest a new house in your favorite neighborhood, go for a walk or drive there when you're in a manifesting mood. Imagine that it's your neighborhood and you're on your way home.

Acting as if is more than mere playing pretend or "fake it till you make it;" it's physical rehearsal for your nervous system. Acting as if can also bring any resistance you have to the surface so you can reparent the part of you that's worried about change. You'll know if there's resistance because trying to act as if will make you feel dysregulated. For example, if you're trying to manifest a relationship and act as if the perfect partner is on their way to you, you might suddenly notice discomfort rising in your body. This is a good time to turn inward and soothe the younger part of you that feels insecure because of past attachment wounding. Remind this part that you're a capable adult who will always take care of it. And then, get back to intentionally acting like the perfect partner is seeking you. This hopeful expectation will have a twofold effect: it will make you alert to potential partners and confident enough to interact with them.

Here's another example. If you're trying to manifest more wealth, you don't have to splurge to act as if. In fact, splurging might make you feel dysregulated (because it decreases your finances) and defeat the purpose of acting as if. Instead, you could read a finance book that makes you feel more prepared to handle larger sums of money. By learning about managing wealth wisely, you'd increase your confidence and let your nervous system and inner parts know that you're ready for more. Remember your reticular activating system? It's the part of your brain that scans your environment and focuses on what's important to you. Acting as if you can handle more money would prime it to look for opportunities to increase your wealth.

Acting as if should generate pleasant, if not expansive, emotions. Living like you've already achieved your dream should feel good. In this state, you're in a manifesting mood; you're strengthening the neural pathways that connect positive emotions and possibility. Do this often enough and it will become your new self-image. You'll start to see yourself as your ideal future self.

If you're skeptical about whether acting as if really helps, consider the recent research on acting. Researchers looked at actors who used method acting to portray characters.[73] Brain scans showed that the actors truly embodied their characters. Their brains changed when they took on different roles. The part of the brain that's responsible for their usual sense of self deactivated, and the part of the brain that's responsible for consciousness showed an increase in activity. By acting like someone else, they were able to suspend their usual identity. After embodying a character for a long time, we also know that actors can struggle to give up some of the habits and traits they've been portraying. This is good news for you. By acting like the person you'd like to become—your ideal future self—your brain can adapt and change too.

Once you begin to act as your future self and your dreams feel like they're orbiting a little closer to your reality, you might have one more common concern. What if you do get what you want, but how it comes is still a shock to your nervous system? This is where asking the Universe for gentle assistance can be helpful.

Ask the Universe to Gently Assist You

When you're feeling dysregulated and anxious, you might still have the fear that when you get what you want, it will be the result of misfortune. This is common for people in trauma recovery. For example, you might worry that if you ask for a new car, your current car will get into an accident and get totaled. These types of fears will subside as you work on creating internal safety. For now, you can ask the Universe for some gentle assistance by ending your prayers, affirmations, or intentions with the following phrase: *This or something better, in a joyful and gentle way.*

You might also be worried that getting something you want will come with a lot of unexpected burdens. For example, if you ask the Universe to help you become a successful musician, you might worry about the downsides of stardom. If this is the case, add the word *thrive* to your manifestation practices. For instance, you can turn the following into a prayer, intention, or affirmation: *Dear Universe, please help me be a successful musician and thrive in all areas of my life. Thank you.*

Once you ask the Universe for gentle assistance, listen for inner guidance. Be willing to strongly consider and follow your intuition, even if you don't see the whole path yet. Guidance is there to help you build a life you love. After all, manifesting in a way that reflects your values and Self is all about thriving, not struggle.

As you develop a greater capacity for trust and master manifesting, you might get to a point where you allow the Universe to determine your goals. This level is definitely more of a trust-fall, but it can be fun once you're ready for it. It involves asking the Universe, or your Self, what it wants you to do and then doing it. When I ask the Universe what it wants from me, the answer I get is almost always a surprise. Most days, when I'm regulated, I'm open and ready to listen. Usually following my inner guidance results in synchronicities that help me or the people I care about thrive. Other times, it leads to something even bigger.

For example, one day when I was driving home, I got the strange urge to drive to the bookstore instead. I followed it thinking the Universe wanted me to buy a book. As I got closer to the bookstore, I noticed a toddler wandering in the middle of the road. She was alone and none of the other drivers speeding by saw her. I acted quickly and was able to help her before she got run over. Once the police arrived, I drove home, without ever entering the bookstore. On days like this, I feel like a little piece to a big puzzle, and it reminds me that goals are more meaningful when they're connected to something bigger.

It took me a long time to get to this place of trusting the Universe's goals. But I'm glad I found my way there. The truth is, I don't want to use my willpower to try to control everything. It's exhausting. And, as it turns out, letting go of control isn't about losing something or sacrificing what you want. It's about dropping into the still, eternal Self that's always been there and allowing it to guide you to what's highest and best—and believing that it's the highest and best. Surrender truly is sweet, but only when you're ready and it's given freely.

So, take all the time you need to turn the practices in this book into habits. You'll grow and begin to trust that it's safe to open to life's possibilities.

Have a Growth Mindset When It Comes to Manifesting

At the beginning of this book, you might have believed that you're not a good manifestor. Maybe it's because you've struggled in the past or because the manifestation strategies you've learned so far didn't acknowledge the true impact of trauma. I hope you're beginning to realize that you're not a "bad manifestor" at all. Your ability to manifest successfully will only grow as you apply what you've learned. I hope you can see that a *fixed mindset*—believing your personal traits are unchangeable—isn't an accurate description of your manifestation abilities.[74] A *growth mindset* means believing you can improve—that you can grow and develop your abilities.[75] Give your brain a chance to rewire and grant yourself time to transform into the version of yourself you've been imagining.

Even if you haven't met all of your goals *yet*, acknowledge the percent closer you are to them, the effort you've courageously shown, the challenges you've overcome, and the transformation you've made as a result. Treat yourself with compassion as you work toward your goals. Just because you're not quite there yet, it doesn't mean you're failing. You're making healthy changes and learning to let go of what's been holding you back so you can feel more vibrant and be more present. You're opening to new possibilities and readier than ever to receive them.

There will still be challenges ahead—days when things don't go as you hoped and times when you feel like a failure—after all, life is still life. Don't get lost in the largeness of your visions of the future. Focus on what you can do today and how you can grow from experiences. Acknowledge feelings of disappointment and frustration and then step back far enough to be able to witness them without judgment. Rather than battling with what's happening, be kind to yourself. When reality falls short of your expectations, there's still a good chance that the perfect thing for you is just around the corner. Too many people give up right before their big manifestation comes through. Don't let that be you!

Be patient with yourself and you will start to look more and more like a self-healer manifestor. Recognizing when you're chasing a wound-based goal because of unmet emotional needs will get easier. Identifying and committing to value-based goals that are aligned with your Self will eventually feel good. Your ability to regulate your nervous system will develop. The habit of doing a you-turn to reparent rather than overfocus on others will also become natural over time. Looking for glimmers and experiencing glows will get easier with practice. Focusing on your goals when you're in a manifesting mood will become the norm. Taking action and reaching those goals will become achievable. Staying humble and grounded when you succeed will be easier because you'll know how to return to Self whenever you stray. Before long, healing will transform your life from one of surviving to one of thriving.

Your Thriving Future

Manifesting is so much more than a way to get what you want. It's a path to empowering yourself. As you learn to manifest, your self-image and what you thought was possible for you will change. You'll start to believe in yourself and create more choices and opportunities in your life. You'll experience a new sense of internal safety and expansion and want the places you live, the job you have, the items you buy, and the relationships around you to reflect your higher values. Regulating, reparenting, and rewiring will get easier because you'll enjoy creating things that serve you.

Through healing, you'll have the power to leave old stories behind because you'll lovingly reparent the younger versions of you who experienced wounds of the past. When you change your relationship with your younger self, new potentials will open up for your future self. Your life will be ready for a new story—one that embraces possibility and expresses your highest self.

After everything you've been through, this is my hope for you. Soften gradually, ever so gently, and you'll find yourself manifesting a future full of love, joy, and abundance. With every step you take, you'll be rewiring your brain from hypervigilance to hope—turning your pain into possibility and your dreams into reality.

Acknowledgments

I feel so much gratitude for my clients, workshop participants, and blog readers. You have been my teachers as I write a guide that honors healing as a part of the manifestation journey.

To the extraordinary team at New Harbinger Publications, thank you. I am so grateful to acquisitions editor Georgia Kolias for enthusiastically believing in this book idea. Your unwavering faith helped it come to life. Jennifer Holder has been a dream developmental editor. I learned so much from your insightful comments and well-honed expertise. To copyeditor Gretel Hakanson—your support and attention to detail made finishing the book a pleasure.

To my amazing colleagues Allison Dorlen Pastor, Abigail Hamilton, and Kristin Jaski—I appreciate your encouragement and friendship. You've always been there for me with a kind word or a good laugh. To my colleague Linda Gresack, thank you for being a wise sounding board throughout the writing process. Your insights about trauma and spirituality were always spot-on.

To my excellent blog and book research assistants Ana Altchek and Misha Meyer, thank you. You remind me how much fun it is to swap manifestation stories and how important it is to bring psychology into the cultural conversation around manifesting.

Finally, I am eternally grateful to my family. To my husband, Damon, thank you for being the best partner and helping me reach my goals. Without your support, writing would have been a dream deferred. To my children, you bring me so much joy and remind me of the importance of presence above all things.

Endnotes

Introduction

1   Vincent J. Felitti, "The Relation Between Adverse Childhood Experiences and Adult Health: Turning Gold into Lead," *Permanente Journal* 6 (2002): 44–47.

2   Arielle Schwartz, *The Complex PTSD Treatment Manual: An Integrative, Mind-Body Approach to Trauma Recovery* (Eau Claire, WI: PESI Publishing, 2021).

3   Schwartz, *The Complex PTSD Treatment Manual.*

4   Janina Fisher, *Transforming the Living Legacy of Trauma: A Workbook for Survivors and Therapists* (Eau Claire, WI: PESI Publishing, 2021).

5   Fisher, *Transforming the Living Legacy of Trauma.*

6   Bessel van der Kolk, *The Body Keeps the Score: Brain, Mind, and Body in the Healing of Trauma* (New York: Penguin Books, 2014).

7   van der Kolk, *The Body Keeps the Score*, 110.

8   van der Kolk, *The Body Keeps the Score*, 110.

Chapter 1

9   Whitney Goodman, *Toxic Positivity: Keeping It Real in a World Obsessed with Being Happy* (New York: TarcherPerigee, 2022).

10   Lucy McGuirk, Peter Kuppens, Rosemary Kingston, and Brock Bastion, "Does a Culture of Happiness Increase Rumination Over Failure?" *Emotion* 18 (2018): 755–764.

11   Steven C. Hayes, *A Liberated Mind: How to Pivot Toward What Matters* (New York: Avery, 2019).

12   Amanda Venta, Carla Sharp, and John Hart, "The Relation Between Anxiety Disorder and Experiential Avoidance in Inpatient Adolescents," *Psychological Assessment* 24 (2012): 240–248.

13   William Mellick, Salome Vanwoerden, and Carla Sharp, "Experiential Avoidance in the Vulnerability to Depression Among Adolescent Females," *Journal of Affective Disorders* 208 (2017): 497–502.

14   Ryan C. Shorey, Michael J. Gawrysiak, Joanna Elmquist, Meagan Brem, and Gregory L. Stuart, "Experiential Avoidance, Distress Tolerance, and Substance Use Cravings Among Adults in Residential Treatment for

Substance Use Disorders," *Journal of Addictive Disorders* 36 (2017): 151–157.

15   Ai Xiong, Xiong Lai, Siliang Wu, Xin Yuan, Jun Tang, Jinyuan Chen, Yang Liu, and Maorong Hu, "Relationship Between Cognitive Fusion, Experiential Avoidance, and Obsessive-Compulsive Symptoms in Patients with Obsessive-Compulsive Disorder," *Frontiers in Psychology* 12 (2021).

16   Holly K. Orcutt, Anthony N. Reffi, and Robyn A. Ellis, "Experiential Avoidance and PTSD," in *Emotion in Posttraumatic Stress Disorder: Etiology, Assessment, Neurobiology, and Treatment*, eds. Mathew T. Tull and Nathan A. Kimbrel (Cambridge, MA: Elsevier Academic Press, 2020): 409–436.

17   Jordi Quoidbach, June Gruber, Moïra Mikolajczak, Alexsandr Kogan, Ilios Kotsou, and Michael I. Norton, "Emodiversity and the Emotional Ecosystem," *Journal of Experimental Psychology: General* 143 (2014): 2057–2066.

18   Lisa Feldman Barrett, *How Emotions Are Made: The Secret Life of the Brain* (New York: Mariner Books, 2017).

Chapter 2

19   Jennifer Breheny Wallace, *Never Enough: When Achievement Culture Becomes Toxic—and What We Can Do About It* (New York: Portfolio/Penguin, 2023).

20   Judith Orloff, *The Power of Surrender: Let Go and Energize Your Relationships, Success, and Well-Being* (New York: Harmony Books, 2014): xvii.

21   Shakti Gawain, *Creative Visualization: Use the Power of Your Imagination to Create What You Want in Your Life* (Novato, CA: New World Library, 2002), 28.

Chapter 3

22   Stephen W. Porges, *The Pocket Guide to the Polyvagal Theory: The Transformative Power of Feeling Safe* (New York: Norton, 2017).

23   Kristin Neff and Christopher Germer, *The Mindful Self-Compassion Workbook: A Proven Way to Accept Yourself, Build Inner Strength, and Thrive* (New York: Guilford Press, 2018).

24   Teruhisa Komori, "The Relaxation Effect of Prolonged Expiratory Breathing," *Mental Illness* 10 (2018): 6–7.

25   Deb Dana, *Polyvagal Theory in Therapy: Engaging the Rhythm of Regulation* (New York: Norton, 2018): 6.

26 Ruth Curtis, AnnaMarie Groarke, Jennifer McSharry, and Michael Kerin, "Experience of Breast Cancer: Burden, Benefit, or Both?" *Cancer Nursing* 37 (2014): E21–E30.

Chapter 4

27 Peter Levine, *In an Unspoken Voice: How the Body Releases Trauma and Restores Goodness* (Berkeley, CA: North Atlantic Books, 2010).

28 Daniel J. Siegel, *The Developing Mind: How Relationships and the Brain Interact to Shape Who We Are* (New York: Guilford Press, 1999).

29 Levine, *In an Unspoken Voice*.

30 Levine, *In an Unspoken Voice*.

31 Exercise adapted from "Step 3. Pendulation and Containment: The Innate Power of Rhythm," from *In an Unspoken Voice: How the Body Releases Trauma and Restores Goodness* by Peter A. Levine, published by North Atlantic Books. Copyright © 2010 by Peter A. Levine. Used by permission of publisher.

32 Jill Bolte Taylor, *My Stroke of Insight: A Brain Scientist's Personal Journey* (New York: Viking, 2008).

33 Willoughby B. Britton, Jared R. Lindahl, David J. Cooper, Nicholas K. Canby, and Roman Palitsky. "Defining and Measuring Meditation-Related Adverse Effects in Mindfulness-Based Programs," *Clinical Psychology Science* 18 (2021): 1185–1204.

34 Cheetah House, "Symptoms," https://cheetahhouse.org/symptoms.

35 Peter Levine, *Waking the Tiger: Healing Trauma* (Berkeley, CA: North Atlantic Books, 1997); Peter Payne, Peter A. Levine, and Mardi A. Crane-Godreau, "Somatic Experiencing: Using Interoception and Proprioception as Core Elements of Trauma Therapy," *Frontiers in Psychology* 6 (2015): 93; Elizabeth A. Stanley, *Widen the Window: Training Your Brain and Body to Thrive During Stress and Recover from Trauma* (New York: Avery, 2019).

36 Eric Gentry, *Forward-Facing Trauma Therapy: Healing the Moral Wound* (Parker, CO: Outskirts Press, 2022).

37 Marie Kondo, *The Life-Changing Magic of Tidying Up: The Japanese Art of Decluttering and Organizing* (Berkeley, CA: Ten Speed Press, 2014).

Chapter 5

38 Richard Schwartz, *You Are the One You've Been Waiting For: Applying Internal Family Systems to Intimate Relationships* (Boulder, CO: Sounds True, 2023).

39 Daniel J. Siegel, *Brainstorm: The Power and Purpose of the Teenage Brain* (New York: Tarcher/Penguin, 2013).

40   Amir Levine and Rachel S. F. Heller, *Attached: The New Science of Adult Attachment and How It Can Help You Find—and Keep—Love* (New York: TarcherPerigee, 2010).

41   Siegel, *Brainstorm*, 163.

42   Richard C. Schwartz, *No Bad Parts: Healing Trauma and Restoring Wholeness with the Internal Family Systems Model* (Bounder, CO: Sounds True, 2021): 130.

43   Lee A. Kirkpatrick and Phillip R. Shaver, "An Attachment-Theoretical Approach to Romantic Love and Religious Belief," *Personality and Social Psychology Bulletin* 18 (1992): 266–275.

44   Lee A. Kirkpatrick, "Attachment and Religious Representations and Behavior," in *Handbook of Attachment: Theory, Research, and Clinical Applications*, eds. Jude Cassidy and Phillip R. Shaver (New York: Guilford Press, 1999): 803–822.

45   Eric D. Role and Julie J. Exline, "Personality, Spirituality, and Religion," in *The Oxford Handbook of Psychology and Spirituality*, ed. Lisa J. Miller (New York: Oxford University Press, 2012): 85–103.

46   Pehr Granqvist and Berit Hagekull, "Seeking Security in the New Age: On Attachment and Emotional Compensation," *Journal for the Scientific Study of Religion* 40 (2001): 527–545.

47   Dacher Keltner, *Awe: The New Science of Everyday Wonder and How It Can Transform Your Life* (New York: Penguin Press, 2023): 7.

48   Zaya Benazzo and Maurizio Benazzo, dirs., *The Wisdom of Trauma* (Sebastopol, CA: Science and Nonduality, 2021).

Chapter 6

49   Eckhart Tolle, "Conscious Manifestation" online course (Eckhart Teachings Inc., 2020).

50   Schwartz, *No Bad Parts*, 130.

51   Schwartz, *No Bad Parts*, 130.

Chapter 7

52   Jay Earley, *Resolving Inner Conflict: Working Through Polarization Using Internal Family Systems Therapy* (Larkspur, CA: Pattern System Books, 2012).

Chapter 8

53   Brenda S. Cole and Kenneth I. Pargament, "Spiritual Surrender: A Paradoxical Path to Control," in *Integrating Spirituality into Treatment: Resources for Practitioners*, ed. William R. Miller (Washington, DC: American Psychological Association, 1999): 179–198.

54 Cole and Pargament, "Spiritual Surrender."

55 Cole and Pargament, "Spiritual Surrender."

56 Cole and Pargament, "Spiritual Surrender."

57 Lisa Miller, *The Awakened Brain: The New Science of Spirituality and Our Quest for an Inspired Life* (New York: Random House, 2021).

58 Tolle, "Conscious Manifestation" online course.

Chapter 9

59 Deb Dana, *Polyvagal Exercises for Safety and Connection: 50 Client-Centered Practices* (New York: Norton, 2020).

60 Exercise adapted from *Polyvagal Exercises for Safety and Connection: 50 Client-Centered Practices* by Deb Dana. Copyright © 2020 by Deborah A. Dana. Used by permission of W. W. Norton & Company, Inc.

61 Dana, *Polyvagal Exercises for Safety and Connection.*

62 Rick Hanson, *Hardwiring Happiness: The New Brain Science of Contentment, Calm, and Confidence* (New York: Harmony Books, 2013).

63 Hyunju Jo, Chorong Song, and Yoshifumi Miyazaki, "Physiological Benefits of Viewing Nature: A Systemic Review of Indoor Experiments," *International Journal of Environmental Research and Public Health* 16 (2019): 4739; Phoebe R. Bentley, Jessica C. Fisher, Martin Dallimer, Robert D. Fish, Gail E. Austen, Katherine N. Irvine, and Zoe G. Davies, "Nature, Smells, and Human Wellbeing," *Ambio* 52 (2023): 1–14.

64 Megan E. Speer and Mauricio R. Delgado, "Reminiscing About Positive Memories Buffers Acute Stress Responses," *Nature Human Behaviour* 1 (2017): 0093.

65 Rollin McCraty, Mike Atkinson, Dana Tomasino, and Raymond Trevor Bradley, "The Coherent Heart: Heart-Brain Interactions, Psychophysiological Coherence, and the Emergence of System-Wide Order," *Integral Review: A Transdisciplinary and Transcultural Journal for New Thought, Research, and Praxis* 5 (2009): 13–114.

66 Joe Dispenza, *Becoming Supernatural: How Common People Are Doing the Uncommon* (Carlsbad, CA: Hay House, 2017).

67 Heather Barry Kappes and Gabriele Oettingen, "Positive Fantasies About Idealized Futures Sap Energy," *Journal of Experimental Social Psychology* 47 (2011): 719–729.

68 Andreas Kappes, Henrik Singmann, and Gabriele Oettingen, "Mental Contrasting Instigates Goal Pursuit by Linking Obstacles of Reality with Instrumental Behavior," *Journal of Experimental Social Psychology* 48 (2012): 811–818.

69   Lucas J. Dixon, Mathew J. Hornsey, and Nicole Hartley, "The Secret to Success? The Psychology of Belief in Manifestation," *Personality and Social Psychology Bulletin* 0 (2023).

Chapter 10

70   Hal Hershfield, *Your Future Self: How to Make Tomorrow Better Today* (New York: Little, Brown Spark, 2023).

71   Hershfield, *Your Future Self.*

72   Austin D. Eubanks, Andrew Reece, Alex Liebscher, Ayelet Meron Ruscio, Roy F. Baumeister, and Martin Seligman, "Pragmatic Prospection is Linked with Positive Life and Workplace Outcomes," *The Journal of Positive Psychology* (2023).

73   Dwaynica A. Greaves, Paola Pinti, Sara Din, Robert Hickson, Mingyi Diao, Charlotte Lange, Priyasha Khurana, Kelly Hunter, Ilias Tachtsidis, and Antonia F. de C. Hamilton, "Exploring Theater Neuroscience: Using Wearable Functional Near-Infrared Spectroscopy to Measure the Sense of Self and Interpersonal Coordination in Professional Actors," *Journal of Cognitive Neuroscience* 34 (2022): 2215–2236.

74   Carol S. Dweck, *Mindset: The New Psychology of Success* (New York: Random House, 2007).

75   Dweck, *Mindset.*

Anna Kress, PsyD, is a Princeton University-trained clinical psychologist with more than twenty years of experience helping people heal past wounds and manifest the life they've always wanted. Her work has been featured in a variety of popular media, and her private practice is based in Princeton, NJ. For more, visit www.drannakress.com.

MORE BOOKS for the SPIRITUAL SEEKER

ISBN: 978-1684035922 | US $18.95

ISBN: 978-1648481970 | US $19.95

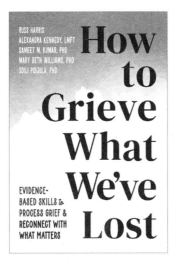

ISBN: 978-1648483196 | US $18.95

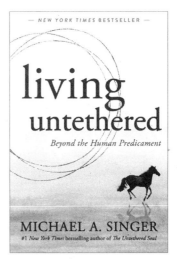

ISBN: 978-1648480935 | US $18.95

newharbingerpublications

NON-DUALITY PRESS | REVEAL PRESS

Did you know there are **free tools** you can download for this book?

Free tools are things like **worksheets, guided meditation exercises**, and **more** that will help you get the most out of your book.

You can download free tools for this book—whether you bought or borrowed it, in any format, from any source—from the New Harbinger website. All you need is a NewHarbinger.com account. Just use the URL provided in this book to view the free tools that are available for it. Then, click on the "download" button for the free tool you want, and follow the prompts that appear to log in to your NewHarbinger.com account and download the material.

You can also save the free tools for this book to your **Free Tools Library** so you can access them again anytime, just by logging in to your account! Just look for this button on the book's free tools page.

+ Save this to my free tools library

If you need help accessing or downloading free tools, visit **newharbinger.com/faq** or contact us at **customerservice@newharbinger.com**.